Remembrances of the Angels

REMEMBRANCES
OF THE ANGELS

50th Anniversary Reminiscences
of the Fire No One Can Forget

JOHN KUENSTER

Ivan R. Dee   Chicago   2008

www.ivanrdee.com

Library of Congress Cataloging-in-Publication Data:
Kuenster, John.
  Remembrances of the Angels : 50th anniversary reminiscences of the fire no one can forget / John Kuenster.
     p. cm.
  Includes index.
  ISBN-13: 978-1-56663-800-5 (cloth : alk. paper)
  ISBN-10: 1-56663-800-3 (cloth : alk. paper)
  eISBN-13: 978-1-56663-816-6
  eISBN-10: 1-56663-816-X
  1. Our Lady of the Angels School (Chicago, Ill.)—Fire, 1958—Anecdotes. 2. Elementary schools—Fires and fire prevention—Illinois—Chicago—History—20th century—Anecdotes. 3. Chicago (Ill.)—Biography—Anecdotes. 4. Oral history—Illinois—Chicago. 5. Fires—Illinois—Chicago—History—20th century—Anecdotes. 6. Chicago (Ill.)—History—20th century—Anecdotes. I. Title.
  LD7501.C434K84 2008
  372.9773'11—dc22   2008017443

This book is dedicated to those who perished,
to those who suffered,
and to those who mourned

Contents

Contents

Acknowledgments

Encouragement and practical assistance came from many sources in helping me assemble these recollections. The group known as the Friends of OLA, including its president Betti (Marino) Wasek, was especially cooperative in providing contacts that in turn led me to more contacts.

My sincere thanks go to all who helped me move these recollections and observations along to their conclusion, including: Joe Murray and Tim Mulcahy, retired members of the Chicago Fire Department; John Raymond, Matt Plovanich, Ron Edington, Connie (Rose) Straube, and Rich Kearney, former students; Sister Mary Lauranne Lifka, archivist for the B.V.M. religious community; Eric Morgan, who set up an informative OLA fire website some years ago; Larry Langford, director of media affairs for the Chicago Fire Department; Nancy Schwartz of the National Fire Protection Association; Michael McAuliffe, fire historian; and Ivan Dee, my publisher, who applied his editorial skills and offered sound advice in guiding the book from start to finish.

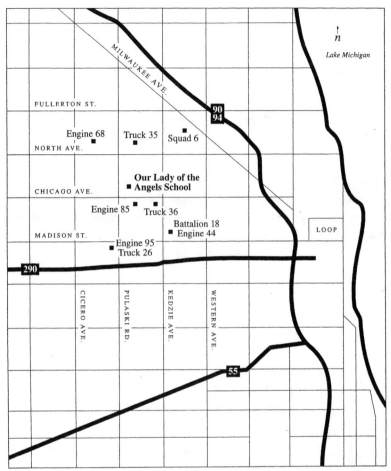

Chicago, showing the locations of Our Lady of the Angels and neighboring fire companies.

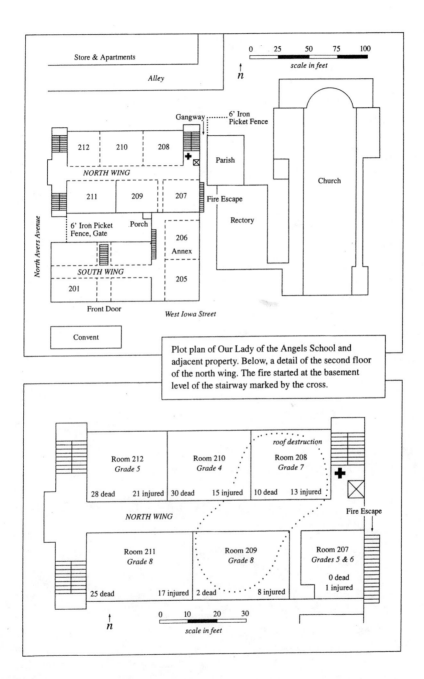

Store & Apartments

Alley

n

0   25   50   75   100

scale in feet

Gangway ········ 6' Iron
Picket Fence

212 | 210 | 208

NORTH WING

Parish

Church

211 | 209 | 207

Fire Escape

North Avers Avenue

6' Iron Picket
Fence, Gate

Porch

Rectory

206

Annex

SOUTH WING

201

205

Front Door

West Iowa Street

Convent

Plot plan of Our Lady of the Angels School and adjacent property. Below, a detail of the second floor of the north wing. The fire started at the basement level of the stairway marked by the cross.

Room 212
Grade 5

Room 210
Grade 4

Room 208
Grade 7

roof destruction

28 dead   21 injured | 30 dead   15 injured | 10 dead   13 injured

NORTH WING

Fire Escape

Room 211
Grade 8

Room 209
Grade 8

Room 207
Grades 5 & 6

0 dead
1 injured

25 dead   17 injured | 2 dead ····· 8 injured

n

0   10   20   30

scale in feet

Remembrances of the Angels

Introduction

❧

The date was December 1, 1958, a cold Monday afternoon just after Thanksgiving when a horrendous tragedy began to unfold in Chicago. Near the city desk of the *Chicago Daily News*, where I worked, rewrite man Bill Mooney stood with a telephone pressed to his ear. Suddenly he yelled, "We've got a school fire on the West Side!"

His alarming shout set off a flurry of activity. With instructions from the city editor, reporters and photographers quickly headed for the back elevators of the building at 400 West Madison Street. A similar exodus was happening at other local newspaper offices and television and radio stations. Media people were racing to reach the scene of a fast-breaking story that would soon command national and international attention. Their destination was Our Lady of the Angels School at 909 North Avers Avenue, some five miles northwest of the Loop.

A fire that produced an enormous amount of lethal smoke had erupted in a basement stairwell in the northeast corner of the school, spreading rapidly to second-floor rooms and hallways, and into a dusty, three-foot-high crawl space beneath the roof. It had gone undetected for some time, and it was not until 2:42 p.m. that the Chicago Fire

Department was notified and sounded the first still alarm, summoning crews of Engine 85, Truck 35, and Squad 6 to the scene.

More than two hundred firefighters from throughout the city eventually responded to quell the blaze and aid in rescue and recovery. The first ones to arrive found a chaotic scene. They struggled to raise ladders to second-floor classrooms where children were trapped or were already jumping from the windows to their death or serious injury. Parents and onlookers watched fearfully to see if their children were safe. Some students could not get out despite the valiant efforts of firemen, who soon began carrying out the dead in tearful scenes.

Ultimately the fire claimed the lives of ninety-two children, ages eight to fourteen, and three teaching nuns. The tragedy shocked the nation, tore apart a community with grief and anger, left many families physically and psychologically scarred for life, and posed long-held questions as to its cause. It also led to a complete overhaul of fire safety standards for American schools.

The consequences of the fire cast a lingering pall over the working-class neighborhood surrounding the school. Residents were largely families of Italian, Irish, Polish, and Slavic heritage who lived in modest homes and conventional two- and three-story apartment buildings. Affected were the lives of seventy-five students who suffered burns while in their classrooms or broken bones in falls or jumps from second-floor windows while trying to escape death. The fire exacted an emotional toll on families who lost a young son or daughter, as well as on immediate relatives, numerous firemen, surviving nuns, policemen, clergymen, reporters, passersby, and local residents who had been eyewitnesses to the disaster. In their grief, many parents accused the Catholic church of incompetent supervision of the school and of attempts to cover up damaging information about the circumstances of the fire.

Responding to reporters immediately afterward, Fire Commissioner Robert Quinn lamented, "If we had had three more minutes, we could've saved them all. We were called too late."

It was years before it could be confirmed that a fifth-grade student at Our Lady of the Angels School had secretly set the fire that led to one of the greatest disasters in Chicago's history, lighting wastepaper in a fiber container on the floor of the back stairwell. He was just ten years old at the time and had no idea his act would take on such terrifying dimensions. Flames ate through the container and spread up through an open pipe shaft beneath a sink, burning inside walls as it moved into a secreted area between the roof and the ceiling of second-floor classrooms. The stairwell also served as a chimney, sucking the fire upward.

Just months after the fire the old Our Lady of the Angels School was torn down. A beautiful new building replaced the fire-ravaged structure in 1960. As years passed, though, the neighborhood declined and so did enrollment at the new school. In the 1990s the school had difficulty maintaining a minimum of 225 pupils required by the archdiocese. It was finally ordered closed in June 1999; the archdiocese planned to locate a charter school in the building.

In December 2006, Cardinal Francis George dedicated the Mission of Our Lady of the Angels at 3808 West Iowa Street, site of the former rectory—"a Catholic presence," said Father Bob Lombardo, "but not a parish." For many years there were suggestions that a marker be placed at the former school site, dedicated to the students and nuns who perished in the fire. A public memorial became a reality on December 8, 2007, and now sits in front of the mission building on Iowa Street. This monument, and its counterpart in Queen of Heaven Cemetery in Hillside, Illinois, where many of the children are buried, remain suitable reminders that victims of the fire have not been forgotten. Yet the most important legacy of those who died can be found in the improved fire safety regulations that govern schools throughout the country today.

This book is not designed to provide readers with a comprehensive account of the Our Lady of the Angels tragedy. For that, readers should consult *To Sleep with the Angels*, the book I wrote with David Cowan, published in 1996. The present book is an effort to recapture some of the memories of this life-changing event upon its fiftieth anniversary. Some of the recollections of the fire itself, by those who were students at the time, are harrowing—and on occasion they offer conflicting views of the episodes in the classrooms, colored by fifty years of memory. My aim is not to reopen old wounds but to see how, a half-century later, the fire has affected the lives of those who were somehow linked to it.

Charles Remsberg

❦

In 1958 he was a twenty-two-year-old reporter working for the City News Bureau, *which serviced Chicago's four dailies, the* Tribune, *the* Sun-Times, *the* American, *and the* Daily News. *A Northwestern University graduate, he has spent his professional life as a writer, including twenty years churning out freelance magazine articles. He has also written several books on law enforcement. Married with four children, he lives in Wilmette, Illinois. The core of what follows comes from a letter he wrote to his parents on December 2, a day after the school fire, recounting his impressions of that afternoon and evening.*

I was the first reporter to arrive on the scene that day. I was assigned to the Traffic Courts building at 321 North La Salle Street and was called by my city desk, telling me that an alarm had come in from a school at Iowa and Avers on the northwest side, and that I should proceed to the location on the chance that it amounted to something.

I took a cab out to the school, and discovered that indeed it amounted to something. The cab could get only within two blocks of the place, so I got out and ran in the direction of the huge column of smoke billowing above the rooftops. All along the way, people were running, some toward the fire, with looks of terror on their faces; others were walking away, guiding groups of children huddled in blankets, looking dazed, wet, and cold.

I came up on the side of the two-winged building that wasn't burning. A boy wearing a school-patrol strap was standing guard at an entranceway there. I asked him what had happened. He said he didn't know for sure, that he heard the fire bell and lots of the kids on the Iowa Street side of the building had thought it was just a practice drill. Then, in the corridors, they had smelled smoke. A few had panicked. On the other side, he said, some had died.

I ran around to the front of the school. The north side of the building looked like a cereal box in an incinerator. Smoke was pouring out of every window, casting a light fog over the ground area and a dense pall above. At the back of the wing, flames still were leaping up. Police were struggling to keep a huge crowd of adults and children back of the fire lines.

After getting a good overall picture of the scene, I headed for the phone. Women in the crowd were hysterical, their faces twisted and wet with tears. Men were holding them back, but they were screaming, "Where are they? Where are they?"

As I passed one woman, she yelled, and her eyes seemed to be focused on a room where her child had been. Other women were fighting with the police. "My kids are in there!" one shouted. "Let me through, let me through."

Some women did break through the lines. They ran up to the front steps of the building facing Avers Avenue, then stood dazed, realizing that the smoke and flames kept them

from entering. They made little, short darts in different directions, like trapped animals. All the while, they screamed and cried.

I pushed into a little grocery store across an alley from the school and asked a woman [Barbara Glowacki] if I could use her phone. She said a fireman was on it. I asked her if she had seen the fire. "Yes. The kids, oh the kids," she said in a thick Polish accent. "They were at the windows and jumping out. I stood there pulling them out of the way as they hit the pavement. Some moved, some didn't. I must have pulled ten away. It was terrible, it was terrible. I can't believe it."

Then I ran to a nearby house, where there was a woman on the porch. I asked to use her phone. She let me in and told me that she too had run to the fire. "All the kids were screaming," she said. "When I saw them jumping, I ran back and got blankets. I've lost some blankets in the deal, but I don't care as long as they helped someone. One little girl came running up to me. She was covered with fire, and the flames were leaping high off her back—even her hair was burning. I wrapped her in a blanket and put the fire out."

After calling the office, I returned to the scene. When I got there the police were bringing out the first body. It was a little girl with a long black pigtail. As the fireman climbed down the ladder with her slumped over his shoulder, her head and arms bobbed up and down with each step. They put her on a stretcher. All the features of her face were still visible, but her skin looked as though it had been roasted. Along her arms, large splotches of skin had come off where the men had touched her, and what was left was reddish brown.

Then they started bringing out other little bodies of helpless kids who had died such horrible deaths. Each time they brought out a body, I made a mark on my pad of paper to keep a tally. I watched them bring out twelve bodies, and each time there were screams from the crowd.

From a second-floor window they lifted the body of a nun. A loud noise erupted from the crowd. "Oh, it's a Sister, a poor Sister," a witness groaned. The nun, like the rest, was carried to a long string of ambulances and police wagons waiting on the street to speed victims to one of the hospitals in the area. The wail of sirens was constant.

I talked with the Fire Department chaplain [Monsignor William Gorman]. "We've brought out twenty-five or thirty," he said. "We don't know whether they're dead or alive, but most of them look like they're goners. There still might be fifteen or twenty inside." I hesitated about phoning in his estimates. They seemed too extreme, but I did, and he was right.

During my second phone call, a rewrite man asked me how I felt about it. "It's terrible," I told him. By the time I got back to the scene, they were bringing bodies out the front of the building, down the school steps on Avers. Firemen were leaning out of the upper windows shouting for more stretchers and blankets. Occasionally a charred hand or a little head with singed hair would be visible under the blankets as they brought out the victims. Some stretchers carried two or more bodies. I began my tally again and made eighteen marks on my pad, one right after another.

Women were breaking through the lines. They kept trying to get to the stretchers and tear off the blankets to see if the dead children were theirs. The policemen fought them back.

My count of bodies carried out from the school rose to thirty-five. They came in a stream as though a huge machine was grinding out little bundles of tragedy.

Water from the school had washed songbooks, tablets, and pencils onto the sidewalk. Near one door was a girl's loafer. The water was an inch deep on my shoes, and my hands were so cold I could hardly write.

When the coroner [Walter McCarron] arrived, he went inside the school and said he had seen one room where there still were twenty-four bodies. He said books were open on the desks and many bodies were huddled by their seats. Others were jammed against the windows. "This is the worst thing I've ever seen," he said. He then issued an order to take all the remaining bodies to the County Morgue.

As firemen brought out three more bodies, I kept wondering what it felt like to carry one of the lifeless forms or touch the charred flesh as these men were doing. I thought what a horrible business they have. At the door a priest stood, administering quick last rites over each stretcher as it was carried out.

I heard the fire commissioner [Robert Quinn] say the fire had shot up the back stairwell and mushroomed over the top of the building. He couldn't understand how it went so fast. He said there was one fire escape at the rear of the building. "The kids tumbled out onto it," he said. He added that many students were caught in fire nets but that many more had jumped to the pavement, some to their deaths.

As other men arrived from the City News Bureau, I was told to concentrate on eyewitness stuff. I talked to a twelve-year-old youngster. He said, "We heard yelling. At first we thought it was someone playing around in the halls. Then we heard someone screaming, 'Fire! Fire!'

11

"I was the last one out of our room, and the smoke was so thick I ran back into the room. I couldn't breathe or nothing. I was about to jump when some girls came in. I told them to get down on the floor because of the smoke. That's what we were told to do in fire drills. The nun didn't say anything about that this time, though. She just said, 'Get up and get out of the door fast.'

"Anyway, we crouched to the floor. Then I threw some books through the glass window and thought again about jumping. I was scared. I kept thinking how I'd look dead. A man came in. I don't know who he was, but he helped the girls out. I could hear firemen outside, shouting, 'Don't jump!' When they got the ladders up, we went down."

In the crowd I found a man who had rescued six kids. He was reluctant to talk and kept mumbling, "I'm tired, I'm tired, leave me alone." But I kept asking him to tell me what happened. Finally, in the confused, stammering sentences of a man shocked by what he had seen and felt, he told his story.

He was walking on the street when he saw the flames. He knew his daughter was in the building and knew right where her room was. He darted in. "I could hear my daughter screaming like hell," he said. "I couldn't get to her. I had to get other kids out of the way first. I grabbed them one after the other and passed them hand by hand to men standing where there wasn't any fire in the corridor between the two wings. At last I could get to my daughter, and I grabbed her by the belly and handed her over. Then I ran out."

In the grocery store next door, the woman I had first talked to was crying. A fireman asked her, "What's the matter? Why are you crying? Your kid got out okay."

"I'm a mother," she said, "and that's why I'm crying. When children are hurt and dead and burning, all mothers are crying." Then she turned to her little pre-school-age boy and sobbed, "Do you know what happened? All your little friends, all the ones that come into the store, are burned up. Remember I told you just today, never, never play with fire. Remember I told you that?" The lad shook his head. "Oh, yes, I did," she wailed. "I told you just today. Now someone lighted a match and all your little friends are gone."

She told me she first learned of the fire when a man came in and wanted to use her telephone to report it. "I ran out," she said, "and saw flames coming from the back of the school. I called the Fire Department, and they said they had sent trucks already. I ran back out, and flames were high on the school. I saw kids marching out the front and heard screaming. I kept wondering where my little girl was. There was pitch-black smoke all over. Then I saw little children at the windows and they started to jump. I grabbed them from the pavement and pulled them over to the side of my building. I know practically everybody in the school, nearly every kid by name. All were screaming for me. I know my girl was in the front classroom. I tried to get to it, but the smoke was too bad. Then, someone told me she got out safely."

I talked to another man who had helped rescue some children. He was coming from the barbershop and thought first of his little girl inside the school. "I ran to the landing on the second floor where her room was. That was as far as I could get," he said. "The smoke and heat were so intense, I had to turn back. Kids were huddled in there and afraid to come out. I guess they were afraid to go down the stairs in the smoke. I couldn't go any farther, so I ran back

down and outside because the first floor seemed like it was already cleared. I hunted for my daughter and son. I heard they were all right and were at some house in the neighborhood. Then, I helped firemen put up a ladder. I climbed up and carried down one girl. Another jumped, and I tried to break her fall with my arms. She knocked my glasses off. Then I went hunting for my kids. Other men had come to help the firemen."

Later I started gathering statistics about the school, its age and condition. I walked inside and looked at one classroom to get an idea of the layout. It was dark, and firemen had rigged a bank of huge spotlights to illuminate the scene. All the bodies had been cleared. People were filing into the church and to Red Cross headquarters set up in the parish rectory.

I was on the story for seven hours, six of them wading in water and debris and pushing through hysterical crowds of parents, and one hour at Franklin Boulevard Hospital nearby. At the hospital I gave my office a list of the names, ages, and addresses of the injured students brought there. After all these years, I still look back on occasion and reflect on the human damage that the fire caused, especially on the anniversary date in December.

Joe Murray

☙

He joined the Chicago Fire Department in 1954 and rode with Squad 6, a rescue unit, to the school fire. He was thirty years old then. As a youngster from a large Irish family that included eleven children, he attended Our Lady of the Angels School, served as an altar boy at church Masses, and like fellow classmates had a crush on Sister St. Canice when he was a third-grader. A widower and now white-haired, he has lived on the Northwest Side of Chicago since 1962. He retired from the department in 1991 as a battalion chief. Both his father, John, and his brother, John Jr., completed their department service as division fire marshals.

Our squad came down California to Augusta Boulevard and then to Hamlin, and we pulled up right behind Truck 36 on Iowa Street. Our run took about four, five minutes. When we pulled up at the school, one of the guys from Truck 36 hollered to me, "Hey, Joe give me a hand, we need this ladder on the other side of the building." Him and I took the ladder over there. Truck 36 had come in just in front of us. They were a box [alarm] truck. We hauled that

ladder about 150 or 200 feet to the corner, and then another 200 feet to the north side of the building.

Kids were jumping out. I weighed about 175 pounds then. What really affected me were two kids jumping down at the same time. A fat kid was coming down head first, and with him a little girl. I had to make a decision on which kid I was going to save. I caught the little girl, and the boy landed right beside me on his head. I always felt awfully bad about that.

We put the ladder up on the alley side of the building to a window of Room 210, and I spent almost all of my tour of duty up there except for a few minutes after the flashover when I left the room and came down the ladder. When it flashed over, I got out of there and went over to the court-yard and I saw a [hose] line lying there. I took it over and took it up the ladder to Room 211 and put the line in there for maybe five minutes. Then I went down and went inside the school. That's about the time I ran into Squad 1 on the second floor of the front stairway. I said to them, "We're going into Room 212 and breach the wall between 212 and 210." And I told the captain, "When you go through the wall and hit Room 210, there's going to be a dozen and a half or two dozen bodies in there."

We breached the wall where the blackboard was, broke the blackboard slate off, and went through that wall. They didn't have to breach the wall to get into Room 212. They went in through the doorway. Guys were working their lines into the hallway. I brought 'em to the left and into Room 212, but there was very little fire in there. I was in fourth grade in that room when I was a student at the school. I was in eighth grade in Room 211, and in seventh grade in 209. My whole family went to school at OLA. I told

one of the firemen, "I know this school and could walk in here blindfolded and know where I was." I knew exactly where everything was. We used to stay after school there all the time, clean the blackboards and stuff like that. Sweep the floors.

When I first started there, it was all boys. It was not coed. In third grade there were finally girls, and that was when I met Sister St. Canice. She was really a pretty young nun, and all the boys, including me, liked her. We had a crush on her. She left OLA for a while but came back later. I didn't know she was one of the nuns who died in the fire until the next day.

Sister . . . her last name was Kelley [Seraphica was her religious name], she was in Room 210. She was lying on top of some kids when we found her. It was like she was trying to protect them. She was larger than the rest of them, so we figured she must be the nun. Later on she was identified as a nun.

I first got into the room before the roof came down. The fire was rolling around the ceiling, coming down maybe six or eight feet, and I stayed down low. I was in there when it started to flash, and when I turned around to go out the window there were two kids lying near the window. I took them and dropped them out the window. And then I went out the ladder and got down. The kids weren't on the ground anymore. Somebody had dragged them away. It was one of the things I never wanted to talk about, throwing the two kids out the window. It didn't sound right.

We got a couple of kids down the ladder first, and then back up there, the ones who were able to get out of the windows were the ones piled on top of other kids. The ones up against the windowsills, they were pinned, and the ones on top of the pile, they were burning. It took me forty-five years before I would talk about it.

There hasn't been one day that I haven't thought about the fire. I had six kids of my own, and the hardest part for me was the next day when I walked in the house, I didn't say anything. I took one look at my kids. . . .

On Squad 6 we never talked about the fire. The guys never said anything to me because they knew it was my school. One guy who wasn't there wanted to go to the Mass for the nuns, but Lieutenant [Jack] McCone said, "No, Joe's going there. It's his school. He's going to the Mass."

I used to wake up at night, sweatin' it. About a week or two later on, I had a dream that was worse than the fire. I dreamt that we had a second fire in the south wing of the school. That south corner was the first part of the school that was built. I told people the school was more of a fire-trap when I went to school there because the south basement was full of discarded furniture. The older north wing used to be the church, but it was converted to classrooms.

I had been a sheet-metal journeyman before I took an exam for the Fire Department in October 1953. I told my boss about the exam, and he said, "It'll be a long time before you get a job on the department. They only take maybe ten, fifteen guys a month at the most." But I got the job on the second call, on January 16, 1954.

I never talked to my wife about the school fire. I never even talked to my father or brother John about it. But the memory of it—and the little kids who died or were hurt—stays with me after all these years. You can't forget.

I think about it almost every day. It pops into my mind, one way or another. The driver of our squad that day was Ray Schaffer. He's dead now. We had acetylene torches, and three different kinds of masks, self-contained masks. We didn't use them the day of the fire. They wouldn't have helped anyway because the masks had pure oxygen and you'd get in trouble in a fire with an oxygen mask.

The only time I talked to Father Cussen, the pastor, was when all the excitement had calmed down. I don't even know if he knew I was talking to him. He was out of it. He was a wreck. He just kept mumbling. He kept saying, "I was over at Dr. Fleming's building"—the one they called Kelly Hall, I think. Dr. Fleming died in 1949 and left all his property on Hamlin Avenue to the church. He was sayin' that's where he was when the fire broke out. I talked to him for a couple of minutes. The next time I saw him was when I went to his wake.

He had a stroke a few months after the fire. I remember when he came to the parish after Father Hynes died in 1936. Later on, I think when I was in eighth grade, he used to deliver our report cards. He'd come in the room and the nun would have the cards sitting on her desk, and he'd hand them out to us. One time I had a pocket full of BBs, and I don't know why I did it, but I threw them on the floor. Then he walked in the front door, stepped on the BBs, and slipped about ten feet. And I never got caught.

After the fire and cleanup work, we got back to quarters just before midnight. I went to bed, got up in the morning, and at roll call we were told we couldn't go home, we had to report to City Hall at nine o'clock and talk to Fire Commissioner Quinn. He wanted to ask us questions. He didn't say much to me. He just asked me my rank and what I did, what I said when we pulled up. I told him what I did, that I followed procedure, that I didn't want to die and wanted to get the hell out of there. I didn't want to talk about the thing any more, especially the next morning. Quinn was a very hard person to talk to. He went after poor Stanley Wojnicki. He was looking for someone to blame. I didn't get home until sometime in the afternoon.

Could there ever be another bad school fire? Well, it could happen again, but maybe a little bit different. When I was in the department I was told you could have fires in similar types of buildings, but they'll never be alike. Atmosphere, temperature, the humidity are seldom the same. You can't predict what a fire will do.

Some memories still haunt me . . . kids jumping out of windows, kids burning to death when they're looking in your eyes. After the flashover and they're all dead, the easy part of the job was taking the bodies out. A lot of people didn't like doin' it, but actually that was the easiest part of that fire for me. After you see youngsters burn to death in front of your eyes and you're barely holding on to them . . . it gets to you and you really don't want to talk about it. You had to be there to understand what was going on.

If you look at the statistics, two-thirds of the fatalities were girls. And two-thirds of the fatalities were the younger kids, the small ones who couldn't get up high enough to get over the windowsill or were pinned against the windowsill where the larger kids were pulling them away and taking their place. I believe there were fifty-six girls who died and thirty-six boys.

Through the years I have gone to the Masses marking the anniversary of the fire. I often think of the B.V.M. nuns who taught me at Our Lady of the Angels . . . how good they were. And I've got to say I never met a nun I didn't like.

Larry Sorce

A senior vice president for investments with the Robert W. Baird Company in Wauwatosa, Wisconsin, he was a thirteen-year-old eighth-grader who was one of the first students rescued from Room 211 on the west end of the school's north wing, overlooking the courtyard. As a young man he spent time in Vietnam and today remains "passionate" about his financial work. Outside of his volunteer duties at local hospices, he is "consumed" with reading material about investments.

That Monday, to the best of my recollection, was cold and sunny with a clear sky. I went to school and got on with the day's activities as usual. I remember looking at the clock that afternoon—it was on the wall right above Sister Helaine's head—and it was about eighteen minutes to three. In only a few more minutes, I realized, we'd be out of school and gone for the day. Then one of our students, who had gone on an errand, came back into the room and said, "Sister, there's smoke in the hall." And Sister got up, went to the door very briskly, opened the door, and the smoke just piled in. She closed the door and the transom above it. Then she put books and I don't know what else at the bottom of the door in an attempt to seal it. But the smoke just kept pouring in.

I was in the second row from the windows and fairly close to the front of the classroom. So I went over to the first window, where there was a student who couldn't quite open it. I helped, and the two of us got it open. Sister Helaine was standing next to me on my right. She was attempting to problem-solve, trying to figure out what we should do. I remember her looking out and seeing the copper drainage pipe that ran down the outer wall at a point that was out of our reach, probably five or six feet away. She was wondering aloud whether we could reach over and shimmy down the pipe—which, of course, was not possible. So we just stood there. I was not in a panic. I wasn't frantic. I was very calm about everything—not that I wasn't afraid.

I kept facing out the window to get some fresh air. In the courtyard a wrought-iron gate blocked the entrance. I saw men on the other side, shaking that gate, trying to move it. They seemed a million miles away, but in reality they were almost within reach. The gate was always locked, and they just couldn't open it. It seemed forever before the firemen got there, but finally they did. I don't remember how they brought the gate down—whether they hit it with an axe to break the lock or what.

Once in the courtyard, they put up a ladder. I think there was one other person who went out the window of our room before I did. A fireman came up the ladder and began the rescues. I remember this intense, intense pressure pushing me up against that windowsill. It came from everybody behind me trying to get to that window. I could not see one inch behind me—it was totally black.

I was short of stature, but I was able to put my leg over the sill, and the fireman, he kinda held on to the side of me as I went down the ladder. His efforts in getting kids out were absolutely fantastic. After going down the ladder and looking behind me when I got a few feet away, at first I didn't see any flames shooting out from my classroom, just this black smoke. Then I saw this flame jump out from the window where I had just been standing. I walked across the street to this old grocery store right on the corner. I'm not sure if I went there immediately or if I just wandered around, kind of aimlessly. But somewhere along the way I picked up a buddy. I don't remember who it was. We ended up walking over to my house. I lived in a two-flat at 920 North Hamlin Avenue, two doors from the back door of the church. My grandmother owned the building, and we lived with her. We were right next to the Stachura family who had a son, little Mark, who died in the fire. At home we grabbed a couple of coats because it was very cold, and we went back outside. At some point I remember standing at that grocery store on the corner of Avers and Iowa. I was outside for a very long time, observing what was going on, most of it alone until my mom and dad found me.

The curious thing is that I don't remember much of what I saw. I look at that as God's way of kind of causing me to blank out what I was seeing. Shocked, whatever. But I have no recollection of seeing any bodies. I don't recall anybody being carried out, I don't remember the violence, seeing any kids jump. And, surely, that all had to be going on before my eyes. I don't know how Sister Helaine got out of the room, but I think she was being a good captain of the ship, trying to get the kids out.

Most of my recollections involve attending the wakes. I remember going to the Armory where they had the Mass for the kids who died. And I can remember looking out my bedroom window at home, gazing at the hulk of the school building that was left before they got to tearing it down.

After the fire I attended a public school, I think it was Ryerson, and then Our Lady Help of Christians where I finished eighth grade. We were bused there. In 1959 I went to St. Mel's High School and later to Marquette University in Milwaukee where I ended up with a political science degree.

I got married in November 1975. I was living in Milwaukee at the time. I had met Judy, a local young lady, and we remained married just shy of thirty years before our divorce. We had one daughter. I now live in Elm Grove, Wisconsin, a suburb about five miles west of downtown Milwaukee.

I keep in touch with a number of friends from Our Lady of the Angels. One of them is Bill O'Brien. We were not of the same class, but we have bonded a lot since the fire. He was in the other eighth-grade class, Room 209. My longest-term friend, Jim Campion, was on the clothing drive that day, so he was not in our classroom. We have stayed close.

For some time I didn't really think much about the fire. It wasn't a daily recollection, it wasn't a stress point for me. But years later it came flooding back. Mine was a very late—I don't know if you want to call it post-traumatic—feeling. It affects me greatly to think about it. I'm not neurotic about it, but I try to attend all the memorial Masses, and when I'm in the neighborhood I'm very interested in showing the area to loved ones. Years and years after the fire, my grandmother sold her building and left the neighborhood, but I don't remember feeling an abandonment of the area. Things, though, definitely changed. There was definitely a different feeling in the community.

I'm of Italian descent. On the roster of students at the school when I was there, Italian names were predominant, but there were many Irish and Polish kids too. The nuns were fantastic people, the priests too, and there was a preponderance of both at OLA. I was very fond of Father Joe [Ognibene]. I talked to him a few days before he passed away.

One of the issues I think about fairly often concerns grief counseling. If you cut your finger on a school playground today, you'll have grief counselors all over the place. That was not the standard back in 1958. Many of the judgments we make about the fire—saying they should have done this, they should have done that—are all made with the benefit of hindsight. In my view it wasn't consciously decided then that we won't do this, we won't do that. It was simply not the standard of the day.

I don't remember ever talking about the fire after that. I don't remember any discussion in the family. It was looked upon as just another event in our lives. It wasn't that it was not consciously thought about, but there was no discussion of it. It very rarely came up.

There's always a positive from a negative, they say. I've had this familiarity with death, not in a morbid sort of way, but without a discomfort about the topic, about the reality of it. I work with hospice stations as a volunteer, and I'd like to think maybe some of that came from this very bad experience at Our Lady of the Angels. I like to be there to provide a little bit of support for patients at the very end. I've been fortunate enough to be there for a lot of friends and family at the end of someone's beloved wife or husband. I never thought in a million years I'd take comfort in doing that, because I was real shy as a kid. I couldn't look you in the eye. I can remember when my dad took me to the barber—I'd keep my head down and cry. Yet here I am today, as a marketing person, a financial adviser, meeting and greeting thousands of people in my life. That's quite a transformation that took place, especially as it relates to life issues, hospice care in particular.

Sister Mary Helaine was a tough teacher, but in a good way. It probably helped me with my military experience. She was a great person. Even though the exit doors in the hallway were outside our room, I never even thought of getting out of the building any other way. It's hard to describe it unless you were in it. This idea of keeping the windows closed, and staying down on the floor where there was no smoke—that at least in my eyes is so foreign to what human nature tells you to do. In the situation we were in, we naturally wanted clean air. So what did we do? We went to the windows, either to open them or break them to get fresh air. We had fifty or more kids in that room. Twenty-four of them passed away.

Some years ago, I tried to track down the fireman who got me down the ladder from my room. I wanted to thank him for what he did. I learned that his name was Charlie Kamin but found out he had died in 1992. I then sought out his son, who had the same name. I wanted to tell him his dad was a great man. But my search was unsuccessful.

I never felt any anger once the fire was over, but I've felt some guilt, wondering why am I here?

Nancy Scanlon Rodewald

❦

She retired as an employee of the Statistical Tabulating Company in downtown Chicago in 1974, the year she married her husband Bruce. "I've been a stay-at-home mother and wife since then," she says. "The nuns at that school were such wonderful people, and good teachers, especially in the three Rs—reading, writing, arithmetic— and geography." A resident of Arlington Heights, Illinois, she adds, "I was one of the lucky ones to escape the fire, frightened but unharmed."

I was sitting in about the fourth desk, in a row right in front of Sister Canice's desk, so it put me almost in the middle of our seventh-grade room [208]. We were getting ready to go home, and Sister was telling us we were going to have some tests later in the week. She got up from her desk—every day at the same time she would get up from her desk, and Patricia, a student in the back of the room, would also get up, and they would both go and open the doors so that we could get our coats.

When Sister went to the front door, she turned the knob and pulled her hand back. Evidently it was hot. She went to grab it again and she pushed the door. When the door was opened there were these huge, black, tumbling clouds of smoke. If you could have seen how thick that smoke was, you wouldn't have wanted to go out in the hallway. That was all you could see. So she immediately closed the door and told us to sit down and pray. And everybody did. I don't know if they prayed, but they all sat down.

We didn't have any lessons about fire survival. We didn't know that you should get down on the floor and crawl, get down where the air was better. We didn't know any of that stuff, so when the nun said to sit, you sat.

Sister kinda stood there. In my memory it kinda goes in slow motion, but I'm quite sure the time went much quicker. As she stood there it started to get a little bit smoky. Little curls of smoke were coming in under the door when the boys asked if they could open the windows, and she said no.

Then some of the kids started standing up. A couple of the girls stood up and started walking toward Sister. I reached in my desk where I kept some hankies—my grandmother always made us carry hankies—and I put a handful of them on my face because it was getting very smoky in there. I kept calling for Sister because it was getting darker in the room. All of a sudden the transoms broke. You could hear the glass shatter. Once that happened, the smoke started pouring in and the boys went ahead and opened the windows.

Then it got very, very dark. I kept calling, "Sister, Sister!" and she answered me once. She said, "Yes?" After that I have little recollection of what happened except I know I started walking toward the back of the room. It was very hard because the desks went from the back of the room to the front, and there was no aisle along the windows. My aisle ended at Sister's desk, which was on a podium. You couldn't get through there. That's all I remember until I was hanging from the concrete window ledge in the very front of the room. I don't know how I got there. I guess I figured I was going to jump. I looked down the length of the building [to the west] and saw kids hanging out the windows. Then some of the kids jumped and some didn't. It was just like they kinda fell, and when they landed, either they weren't moving or this one girl, she just kinda bounced. I later learned she was Charlene Campanale. She broke her back in the fall.

At that point I was just not gonna let go. I found out later on that I had moved hand over hand on the window ledge to let one of the boys out. He told me that about ten years ago, and I was really surprised. He told me his name was Jimmy Luberda, and he thanked me. Finally somebody, a gentleman, came down the alley with a ladder, and he and another man put the ladder up. I guess I was the only one hanging there, and they got me down first. I had to stretch my legs to reach the ladder. I was able to touch the first rung with my toes. I was about five feet two then. I have no recollection of how cold it was. When I got down, parents were already pulling kids who had fallen away from the school building and sitting them up against the wall of the candy store next to the alley. I know there were a lot of kids at the windows, all of them yelling and screaming. I ran across the street [Avers] and found one of the nuns from another class, and I asked her, "What should we do?" She said, "I don't know."

I ran back across the street, and one of the girls from my classroom threw me her wallet from the upper window.

Emily. I guess it was very important to her. Luckily she did get out. I stood there for a little while longer, and then I decided to go home. By the time I got around to the other side of the building, at the corner, that's when I finally saw firemen. They were laying out their hose line. On Iowa Street I remember it was chaos in front of the church. All the parents were coming and a couple of mothers grabbed me, asking me, "Did you see my son? Did you see my daughter?" Then I just ran all the rest of the way home.

We lived in a two-flat on the 900 block of Monticello, a few blocks east of the school. My grandparents lived on the first floor, and we lived on the second. My mother happened to be home because she had just come from the hospital with my baby sister. I also have an older sister who was a freshman in high school then. Now I also have a younger brother, but at that time there were only my two sisters and myself.

My mother had been on the telephone, talking to one of her sisters, and when I rang the doorbell, I really laid on it. When she saw me, she could tell I was upset. She couldn't understand what happened to me. I had no coat, I was freezing, and I smelled really bad from smoke. I told her there was a fire at school. She had me change my clothes, made me some tea, and called my dad right away.

That fire spread so fast. At 2:30 every afternoon, two of the girls from my room would go down that rear staircase to the first floor to help first-graders in the room below us put their coats on. They went down that staircase at 2:30 that day, but they obviously didn't see anything because the fire door on the first floor was closed.

Later my life took a funny turn. I married a firefighter, Bruce Rodewald. In fact he's a third-generation firefighter.

Both of our sons are firefighters. My older son, Kurt, is a fireman/paramedic in Mundelein, and my younger son, Craig, is a full-time fireman in Mt. Prospect. My husband was born and raised in Arlington Heights and was fire chief there for more than twenty years. He retired a couple of years ago. He explained a lot to me, because I wasn't real fond of firemen when I first met him. We got married in 1974.

All these years after the school fire, do I think about it much? Does it come back to me? Oh, yes, it does. It really upset me that they never did anything at the school. As students we could never mention the fire. It was just understood that we weren't allowed to talk about it. It was like they wanted to sweep it under the rug, and you just went on with your life. No one questioned the church. People today, they question everything, but in those days they didn't. I was happy they finally put up that memorial to the nuns and kids in front of the old rectory. It's a shame it was done so awfully late because a lot of the people are gone, especially the parents. It took a terrible, terrible toll on the families.

Sister Canice was very, very calm during the fire. We all have different reactions when something like that happens. My very best friend, Lorraine Nieri, who sat a couple of rows over and one seat ahead of me, had come to the school that fall. She was just sitting there with tears coming down her face. She didn't say anything. She didn't get out. Neither did the girl in front of me.

In the room next to ours, Sister Seraphica had the fourth-graders. She taught me in an earlier grade and was a real sweetheart. When I heard the story that she told those kids to put a piece of paper in their mouths so they wouldn't bite their tongues when they jumped, I could see her doing that. She was feisty. I could see her wanting to get her kids out. We heard that story about the paper right away, within days of the fire.

My best friend who died, Lorraine, I've always kept in touch with her family all these years. When Mrs. Nieri died a few years back, I went to the wake and was talking to one of Lorraine's aunts. We were reminiscing a little bit about Lorraine, and I was saying we used to have these contests to see which of us could bite our fingernails down the worst. And her aunt looked at me and said, "When we buried her, she had no fingers." It was really hard to hear that because you don't want to remember anybody that way. You want to remember them the way they were before.

It was so hard when we went to funerals for days. The funeral homes were so crowded, and they had tiny little rooms where they were trying to accommodate everybody. Some of the kids being waked looked like they were sleeping, with not a mark on them. Others had to have closed caskets. I remember the little boy who lived just a few doors away from us—he went out the window, but he broke his neck. He lived for just a couple of days, and then they said there was nothing else they could do.

After the fire we went to Our Lady Help of Christians School for just a short time, and then we went to Cameron, the public school. It was a little hard there because we were on the third floor. That fear of fire never leaves you. Every time I go somewhere today, the first thing I do is check where all the exits are. And I do not like crowds or closed-in spaces.

I think the nuns on our side of the building were unfairly criticized for not getting their students out through the hall. There's no way they could've let us go out there. There really wasn't. They did the best they could. I think they had never considered anything like that happening. Who would ever have thought of a scenario like that? What I worry about is that people will forget and that it will happen again.

After all these years, I don't want anybody to forget what happened so long ago, because I don't ever want another child to go through something like that. It's there for all the rest of your life. It's a part of me, and I'm sure it has shadowed every decision I've made in my life.

Rosemary Pisani Bieker

✿

A perky housewife and grandmother, she lives some seventeen hundred miles from the West Side neighborhood in Chicago where she came of age. She recalls fondly her years at Our Lady of the Angels School and remains grateful for the friendships she has maintained through the years with former classmates. She was rescued from the fire without injury.

I lived a block from the school at 814 North Avers, near Chicago Avenue. I don't remember much about the morning of the fire except that it was cold. We had gone to my cousin's birthday party the day before. I was in eighth grade, Room 209, on the second floor. The room was on the south side of the school's north wing. In the afternoon, probably about twenty after two or two-thirty, we were doing math, some kind of an assignment Sister Davidis had given us. I can remember looking at the clock, thinking, "Oh, I wonder how much time I have left to do this?"

Then, all of a sudden this boy in the back of the room . . . he had come from Italy, so he was a little older—I was thirteen and he was probably fifteen or sixteen—because he didn't speak the language so well . . . he said, "Sister, it's hotter than hell back here!" I was shocked when he used the word "hell." At that time it was a word we weren't supposed to use when expressing ourselves; now it means nothing. Sister Davidis said to him, "Open the door." As he opened it, all this black smoke came in. So Sister said, "Okay, get your books and put them around the bottom of the door. If the smoke gets too bad, get down on the floor." The part that shook me up a little bit was when she said, "Let's start praying." Maybe we said a Hail Mary, but that was it. Sister then said, "Get to the windows."

I went to the window, and then I remembered that my purse, my wallet, and my library book were still on my desk. I sat in the middle of the room near the back, a few rows from the windows. I went back to my desk to get the book that was due at the library. I never anticipated what was about to happen. Sister told me, "Get back to the window." So I just dropped the book and got to the window. One girl, I remember, was screaming hysterically, and Sister just slapped her a little across the face because she was getting everybody else all worked up.

I was at the back window with a couple of my friends, including Rose Tortorice and other students. We saw Father Ognibene and Sam Tortorice, the father of Rose, reaching out for us from the annex part of the building. A couple of boys got out first. They just jumped onto the overhang above a door of the annex. A couple of girls might've gone out before me. I was next in line. When I got up on the sill, there was a pencil sharpener there and my skirt got caught on it. Somehow it came loose, and Father Ognibene and

Sam Tortorice lifted me out of the window. I didn't have to jump into their arms. They just lifted me to another window in the annex, and I ran down the stairs to Iowa Street. At that time not many people were out on the street because a lot of students were being sent to the church.

I went to the church, and when I came out later there were tons of people on the street. My mother came—I was the oldest of three girls—and asked me, "Have you seen Pattie?" My sister Pattie was in second grade. I said, "No, I haven't." But she had gotten out early and come home safely. She had thought it was a fire drill when they left school. We were all home, and shortly after that the doorbell rang. It was the mother of my good friend Rosalie Guzzo, who was in my classroom with her twin brother Frank. Mrs. Guzzo was going to take them to the hospital to be checked. I had black smoke in my nose, but I was not injured. She said, "Do you want to come?" And I said, "Oh, no, I'm fine." I remember I went back down the block to the school a couple of times to look, but I never went to the side where my classroom was. It was just pandemonium there.

At home my younger sister was watching TV when they interrupted a program to announce the name of a girl, Kathy Hagerty, as one of the first to be pronounced dead. She was in Room 211. I remember she had asthma really bad, and that may have figured in her death. When I heard her name and that she was dead, I just couldn't believe something like that was happening. That night we must have gotten ten phone calls from my friends or parents asking, "Do you remember seeing Nancy?" "Do you remember seeing Eileen?" You couldn't put together the severity of it all.

I was about five feet one or two in eighth grade. There weren't many of us who were tall in that class. I had known

Father Ognibene before the fire, but I never really talked to him about it later. My dad was an auto mechanic and knew him pretty well because Father Ognibene was the priest at church responsible for the Italian Catholic Federation. My dad was involved in that. He was working the day of the fire. A lady in the office said to him, "Bill, what school do your kids go to? It's burning." He freaked. There were no cell phones, of course. He quickly got in his car and raced home. He worked in Old Town, I think at Wells and Division, where his garage was. So he had a long trip home.

That evening the parents of my classmate Michele McBride, who lived right across the alley from us, came over asking, "Did you see her? Where was she?" I couldn't remember if I had seen her outside the room or not. Everything was so jumbled up in my mind, but I later learned Michele was severely injured.

The next day—we did not get the newspaper delivered to our home at that time—my mother said to me, "Why don't you get the newspaper." I went across the alley to a place called Goldie's and bought the newspaper, and on the front page were the pictures of all these school kids who had died. They were all kids I knew. I really had not anticipated such a tragedy. I had gotten out and didn't know the roof had collapsed, because I hadn't gone back to that part of the building. But the horror of it set in on me.

I remember then going with my parents to wakes for different children. Some of them looked like they were sleeping; they hadn't been burned. A group of us girls went to visit two families who had lost their daughters. We saw the parents of Nancy Pilas because we were very close—we belonged to a club that would meet at each other's homes. And we visited Eileen Pawlik's mother. That was very difficult. Both girls were also eighth-graders in the room next to ours, Room 211. It seemed like everybody you knew had a young brother or sister who had died.

Gerry Andreoli, in our room, was burned badly. When he first came home from the hospital, I went with five or six kids to visit him at his home, where his father showed us a book with pictures of Gerry's treatment when he was in the hospital. I don't know how much good our visits did, but they were a way of showing our support and unity. Our hearts were in the right place.

After the fire—I think it was the following Monday—we were sent to different public schools. I went to Orr school. A couple of the nuns were there. One time the fire alarm went off by accident, and a few of the kids really freaked. I was the kind of person who tried to be not tough, but brave it out. We would always walk from Orr back to Our Lady of the Angels when we were practicing for our graduation. The graduation was held in the church, and some of my classmates who were hurt in the fire were able to come. At the time there were no grief counselors. The priests said, you just have to get on with your life, and don't think about it. Since my immediate family was not affected by the loss or injury of a child, you just kind of went on.

I know the neighborhood changed. A lot of people moved out after the fire, and I don't blame them one bit, especially if they had lost a child. But we stayed until I was a sophomore in Siena High School. Then we moved from the area.

Every December 1 I think about the school fire. After I got married in 1967, my husband and I were in Germany for six months, and then we moved to Portland, Oregon. So

assumed that one of the rooms was having a Christmas party. That would have been a fair assumption at that time of the year.

Sister didn't panic. She remained very calm. She immediately went to the back door to try to open it and realized she had forgotten her key at the convent. Apparently they kept that door locked because some boys would pull the fire escape down, access the school building through that door, and vandalize. In a very short time the smoke became thick and black. The heat broke that transom above the front door. Quickly Sister had some of the boys stand on the desks and try to break the skylight with books, but they were not successful. It's probably a good thing they didn't, because I'm sure that would have allowed more oxygen in the room and would have made the fire spread faster.

Then I remember a lot of the children at the windows. I couldn't get to a window. When it was becoming very dire, Sister went to the back of the room where there was a tall metal cabinet. In that cabinet were stored clean rags, erasers, and other supplies. She had another girl and myself grab the clean rags and distribute them to other children to put over our faces.

The room became so filled with black smoke you couldn't see anything. Sister instructed us to lie on the floor. She threw a plastic flowerpot out the window, and that's how she caught the attention of Father Hund, since our room was so close to the rectory where he had been resting in a second-floor bedroom.

I was the last child to leave our room after Father Hund and the janitor, James Raymond, opened the back door. Until that point, though, when we were lying on floor, I knew with certainty that I was going to die. I prayed to the

Blessed Mother and asked her to spare me for the sake of my mother and father, because I knew they would not be able to come to grips if I had died in the fire. When I had gone home for lunch that day, I had begged my mother to allow me to stay home. I even faked a stomachache. My mother told me to go to school and if I was still feeling sick, then come home. When I was on the floor of the room, the thought came to me that my mom would never forgive herself for forcing me to return if I had died that afternoon.

I was on the sixth-grade side of the room, near the west wall. The fifth-graders were on the east side, closer to the windows. While we were still in the room, though it was black with smoke, you could see kind of an orange haze and could hear the fire crackling, consuming the desks and wood. Without a moment to spare, they got that back door open. I was starting to feel woozy. Even though I had been lying on the floor, I was starting to lose consciousness. As the last one out the back door, I was terrified to go down the fire escape. The stairs were very steep, very intimidating to me. I thought I'd fall all the way down. Flames were pouring through the windows when a kind fireman put his arm around me and said, "You'll be fine, honey. Just duck your head under the fire and you'll be all right."

When I got to the bottom of the stairs, Father Joe was standing there, and he recognized me immediately. Our family was pretty close to Father Joe. He picked me up—he was so tall compared to me—and he just crushed me to his chest, sobbing. He was crying so hard, and to this day I can still feel his tears running down my cheek and my neck. He set me down on the ground and instructed me to go to the church and find Sister Geraldita and my classmates, which I did. Then I remember sitting together with my class. I was perplexed, wondering what had happened. Naturally I didn't know the extent of the fire. When we were released to go home, oddly enough I don't remember feeling cold walking home without a coat. I lived at 717 North Hamlin Avenue, a little bit south of Chicago Avenue.

When my mother saw all the smoke and all the fire equipment going in the direction of the school, she knew immediately it was the school. So she and my older sister, who had been home sick that day, bundled up and hurried over to the school. My mother saw people there and asked them if they had seen me. No, they hadn't. She became very concerned. My father was traveling nearby, and the traffic was all backed up when a truck driver leaned over and shouted to him, "Do you know that OLA school is on fire?" My dad worked at Pyle-National, a factory near Kostner and Division. He left his car and ran all the way home. When my dad discovered I was not home yet, he fainted. My sister stayed at the school and sent my mother home, because my mother had given her coat to a younger cousin who didn't have a coat. My sister helped distribute blankets to some of the children who were evacuated from the school.

When I finally got home, my mother called our family physician because my mouth and nose were so blackened from the smoke. He recommended that I get into a cold shower. Later that day became very surreal as we watched television and saw the list of names of the children who at that point were deceased. That night we all went to bed. My sister and I shared a bedroom, and I woke her up in the middle of the night and said, "I smell smoke." She said, "No, no, it's just what happened today. Go back to sleep." I said no, and so I got up and woke my parents. They immediately got out of bed, turned on the light, and saw that the apartment was filled with smoke. We had just converted from coal heat to natural gas heat, and the new motor had burned out, sending smoke up to the second floor where we lived in a two-flat building. My grandparents lived on the first floor. It scared the wits out of me. Without waiting for anybody, without putting on a coat or shoes, I ran down the front stairs to the porch.

After the school fire we went to Our Lady Help of Christians for a short time. That's where Sister Geraldita had a nervous breakdown in the classroom, right in front of us. Although we were young kids, we didn't know what was happening to her. That was very frightening. And then I went to John Hay public school and after that to Siena High School. Following high school I was eager to be cosmopolitan, get into the working class. I did not want to pursue college, which I regret now. My first job in high school was at St. Anne's Hospital in the medical records department. So I had access to many of the records of the OLA children who had been taken to St. Anne's.

I have to say that I probably came away from the school fire with fewer emotional scars than others. It strengthened my faith while I know it diminished others', but then again I didn't lose a sibling or a close relative in the fire. I'm cognizant of the fact that I do not like being in crowds. If I'm in an arena type of environment, I almost get panic attacks. Even going to a movie, the first thing I do is look for an exit. I have a friend, Robert Nedza, who was a classmate. He became a clinical psychologist and interviewed a number of us from the class of 1961 because he was doing a thesis on post-traumatic stress syndrome. This was a few years ago. After his findings and interviews, he wrote me a letter and told me he was pleased to say that no one he interviewed exhibited any signs of that disorder. We were in the first graduating class at OLA after the fire.

I pretty much knew how the fire happened. At least the speculation was that a fifth-grade boy had set the fire. It didn't take long for that rumor to go around, and I believed it. To this day I believe it. He was a strange kid, but in my heart of hearts I still can't believe he intended that ninety-two children and three nuns should die.

My folks, both of them Italian, stayed in the neighborhood until about 1970. My father lives with us and turned ninety-two in 2008. My parents encouraged me to talk about the experiences I had in the fire. I couldn't understand why other parents didn't want their kids to talk about it. After the fire my dear friend John Raymond [a fifth-grade student in Room 212 who escaped the fire by leaping out a window] and I have talked to each other a great deal. I guess we have our own therapy, but I have stayed in contact with many of my classmates from sixth grade and still maintain close friendships.

Admittedly the fire tore the old neighborhood apart, but it also brought all of us who went through it much closer together. In retrospect it was a double-edged sword, both a curse and a blessing. I'm sure today, had it not been for the fire, many of us would not have such close feelings for one another.

Ken Sienkiewicz

❦

Through the encouragement of his wife Rebecca, he finally
was able to unburden himself of the sense of guilt he felt
from surviving the fire because of his absence from school
while two of his best friends died. His perspectives on life
and death have been tempered by emotional trials, including
the separation and divorce of his parents when he was
young, his mother's later hospitalizations, his own divorce,
and the responsibility of helping care for a handicapped son.
He lives with his wife and son in Lombard, Illinois.

Back in those days I had asthma, and my mother always
would keep me home one extra day after I had an attack
to be sure I was okay. It seemed that I had an asthma
attack—not being able to breathe—every other month. On
the "extra day" for me that month, the OLA fire broke out.
So I was at home watching TV. I'm not sure how I heard
about the fire, but I got my coat on right away and ran like
a banshee toward the school, watching the smoke rise in
the sky. We lived in a four-story apartment at 1105 North
Central Park. I was an only child. My parents had been
separated since I was three or four and were in the process

of a divorce at that time. When I got to the school I watched all the action from the alley side. That's where my room [212] was—Sister Mary Clare Therese's room.

My recollection is that I saw a couple of kids jumping and missing the net and others being carried down ladders from the room. My two best friends, John Manganello and Larry Dunn, were fatalities. John jumped and came down feet first, and his body just crumpled when he hit the ground. Larry was taken down on a ladder. I'm not real clear how long I stayed there. I remember getting back home but don't know what time it was.

John and I used to smoke together. That's how our friendship started. There was a group of guys who would go through the back door of the school and have a cigarette outside, near that concrete trash retainer close to the alley. John and I were among the kids who did that. Can you imagine at that age? But in those days almost every adult was smoking, and the kids would take a cigarette or two from a pack lying in the house of their parents, aunts, or uncles and try them out. Larry was more than just a friend that I talked to in the hallways or in our room. He and I were chums, but there wasn't much extracurricular activity we got into. We just kinda hung out together. He lived on Grand Avenue and came from a big family. John lived on Ridgeway. We were fairly close to each other that way. Jim Moran "The Courtesy Man" had an automobile agency on the corner of my block, at Grand and Central Park. He sponsored the Saturday-night movies on TV. We played ball in a lot that was right next to where he parked all his cars. We were sort of like his guardians, and if we saw somebody screwing around with his cars, we'd go spook them with baseball bats. Then we'd go tell Moran and he'd buy us a Coke.

Since the death of my friends, John and Larry, I've always wondered, "Why them and not me?" I was angry that Sister Mary Clare Therese didn't get those kids out into the hallway and down the front stairs—at least give them a chance that way. Their chances of dying in the room versus dying in the hallway were fifty-fifty.

But I wasn't there. If I had been, I can't say that I would have led some charge down the stairs. Sister Mary Clare was a quality person. This is not a reflection on her as a person but on what she might have done differently. It was just crappy training. The Catholic school system at that time did not seem to have any evacuation plan, any disaster plan. It was like "God will take care of you." Well, bullshit. God won't take care of you in a situation like that. You need to open the door and run your ass down the stairs. If thirty kids die out of sixty, it's terrible. But if fifty kids die out of sixty, it's more than terrible. That's a travesty. In the public schools they don't have the same expectations of help from a higher source in times of trouble. Maybe my view might be challenged as a case of second-guessing because the fire had such a head start and was unnoticed for so long. The person who started the fire was goofy. We all knew that. What he did gnawed at me for years.

We moved a year after the fire. I had gone to Our Lady Help of Christians School to finish out fifth grade. For seventh and eighth grades I went to St. Ferdinand on West Barry Avenue. Later I went to St. Patrick High School at Belmont and Austin. After graduating from there in 1966, I did some Wright Junior College and took classes at Triton College, never graduating with a diploma but spending five or six years going at night. I took courses that I thought would benefit me. In today's world, without a degree you're an idiot.

I have been married thirty years to my lovely wife Rebecca. I married my first wife, a schoolteacher, in 1970. That marriage lasted a few years, and we had a friendly divorce. I have three children. My oldest daughter Cori Rose has a grandson. My son Mark is mentally handicapped. He's autistic, nonverbal. He lives with us and will live with us until we die. For not getting killed in the fire, I thought I was going to be kissed, but I really wasn't. I'm proud of my son; I don't hide him. I take him everywhere. I love him. My youngest daughter, Kristi, who's twenty-three, went to USC in California to get a degree in film, and she's now handling insurance for an ambulance company. My life, it really hasn't been too bad. It could have been a lot worse.

In looking back on the school fire after fifty years, a lot of things I originally thought are now sort of blurred in my memory. I'm not sure that what I heard after the fire is what I actually saw there. I was so traumatized. There was so much shit going on—kids jumping, people dying. What you see is so horrific that your mind can't handle it, and you sort of blot out some of it. It was some terrible stuff. I would never want to put my name on a piece of paper and say, I saw this or I saw that. But one thing that stays with me is the firefighter carrying a young kid out. He was carrying Larry Dunn in his arms.

In retrospect the only good that came out of all those kids dying is that our schools are safer today. That's their legacy.

One of my kids better be a president or better be something because in that room I should have died. Somewhere, somehow, one of my siblings should make some significant contribution to the world. If not, why was I spared? I have no idea. It's a rhetorical question. There's no answer for it. I'm sure there's a whole bunch of people who lived through the fire and have thought, "I didn't die. Why?"

My wife has been bugging me for twenty years to get this out of my system. I'm sketchy on a lot of stuff that happened during the fire, but I do remember so much afterward—all the wakes and funerals, all the dead kids. It was devastating to go to the wakes, one after another. It was one of the toughest weeks I ever went through in my life. You couldn't get it out of your mind. A lot of them were closed caskets, which made it worse—leaving you wondering how badly someone had been hurt.

Ninety-five lives was a bitter price to pay for better safety precautions in schools, but sometimes that's the only way we learn to prevent further tragedies.

Jim Grosso

❦

A resident of Oak Park, Illinois, he and his wife Mary have three sons, "all out on their own, thankfully." For many years the school fire left him with bad feelings about his childhood, until he learned about the Friends of OLA, an organization through which he has reconnected with former students. In making those connections, he has been able to achieve a more positive attitude toward his grade-school days.

I was in Room 206, sixth grade. We hung all our coats in a narrow passageway that separated our room from Room 205, where all the kids got out, going down the back fire escape. My teacher was Miss Pearl Tristano. I'm not sure where I was sitting that day, but what I do remember is that at least once a day a couple of the boys would be designated to take the trash down to the basement. On that day, when we were coming back upstairs after dumping the trash in a drum outside the boiler room, we started to see and smell smoke coming from the north wing. We alerted our teacher. She left the room for a short time, then came back, got us all lined up, and took us down the stairs and out the Iowa Street door.

I very vividly remember Miss Tristano going to the fire alarm and pulling it. I know there was some question later on about whether it actually rang or not. I don't remember hearing the bell, but I distinctly remember her setting it off as we left.

When we got outside, some of the kids were told to go into the church, but others of us were told to head on home as quickly as we could because we hadn't had time to get our jackets or coats. We were there in our shirtsleeves. I started to run toward home because it was so cold. Actually, I didn't go straight home. My father George was a plumbing contractor. He had a plumbing and heating store on Chicago Avenue and Lawndale. I ran over there first and let him know what was going on. Then I went home. We lived in a two-flat at 739 North Trumbull, about a mile away. When I got home my mother first heard about the fire from me. She was relieved I made it home safely. Then she got on the phone and started calling around to get more information, and turned on the radio. When I heard the news on the radio and later on television, it was kind of a shock to me. What happened totally enveloped our lives for the next weeks and months.

It didn't take long until all the rumors about how the fire was set began to float around. They involved a boy in our class. Everybody thought he was kind of weird, just a strange kid. I believe he died about a year and a half ago.

Our family is of Italian descent. I had an older sister who was in high school then, and I had two younger brothers. One of my brothers was in kindergarten in another OLA building, and the other hadn't started school yet. I went to Our Lady of the Angels all eight years. I graduated in 1962.

I had mostly nuns in grade school. From an educational standpoint, my impression of grammar-school days is excellent. For the rest of my educational career through high school and college, I was told several times by the teachers how good my skills were—language skills, composition, and all that. I say that with thanks to the good Sisters. I went to Fenwick High School in Oak Park and then to Loyola University on the North Side of Chicago. Our family moved from the old neighborhood to Itasca, Illinois, in 1969, after my high school years.

After all these years, I don't think my feelings about the school fire are unique. I have talked with other former students who had the same sort of experience that day. After the fire, it's like my entire time in grade school had a negative connotation—feelings of anger and guilt and sadness. The fire colored my whole memory of childhood, and my wife would always ask me whenever the subject would come up, "Why don't you ever talk about that?" I'd say, "I really don't know why. I just don't want to."

They built a new school and it was safer, but it just seemed that somebody should have done more before the fire happened, and that they could have done more afterward. My feeling of anger came from that perception. There was no counseling afterward. The teachers and other people in the neighborhood told us to forget about it.

Then, after reading the book *To Sleep with the Angels*, and when the OLA website was set up, I got back in touch with former students that I hadn't really had much to do with for thirty or forty years. All of a sudden, after feeling bad about my childhood my whole life, I started to feel good about it again . . . talking to people, seeing that we all turned out okay after all. It was great, very therapeutic. I keep in touch at the annual reunion dances, and I've gone to the memorial Masses each year.

I still have a sense of gratitude to Charlene Campanale, who got the Friends of OLA organized again. She was motivated, friendly, and could make things happen without stepping on anyone's toes. What she did got me in touch with everybody and enabled me to feel good about my childhood again. Charlene broke her back and pelvis when she jumped from her fourth-grade room, and spent three months in the hospital. She died in 2003 of a brain aneurysm. She had been a special education teacher and was married to Wayne Jancik.

In the old neighborhood we played sports the year round. We played Little League baseball all summer. Then we played football, and after football we played hockey. Although Little League was organized, a lot of other games were just pickup. We played at Kells Park at Chicago and Kedzie. In the winter they'd freeze it, have an ice rink, and we'd go there and play hockey. Those are fond memories. The spare jobs I had as a kid were cutting lawns, shoveling snow, and I was a bag boy at the local grocery for a while.

I served as altar boy for a couple of years at Masses offered by Father [Alfred] Corbo, Father Ognibene, and Father Hund. Father Corbo, he was funny, he'd always be cracking a joke. Father Ognibene was always so nice and warm. He had such a warm personality. It was a close community in those days. The big carnival in the neighborhood every year was originally staged by the Alamo American Legion Post. After Alderman Pat Petrone died, they changed it to the Petrone Post, but they put on a carnival at the corner of Pulaski and Chicago that many parishioners attended. That was always a lot of fun.

The fire had such an impact on so many of us, but it did not affect my faith, not consciously. Maybe the discipline we encountered in grade school had something to do with that. We had about fifty-five kids in our room. With that many kids in most rooms, the teachers had no choice but to use strong discipline. What makes me happy now, though, is the memorial for the deceased nuns and students that has been placed near the site of the old school and also the memorial garden that honors Father Ognibene at Our Lady Mother of the Church parish on West Lawrence Avenue, where he once served as pastor. I've driven by there, and it's nice to see that Father Joe has not been forgotten.

In fact, none of us should forget what happened so many years ago to so many innocent kids and good people.

Emily Ruszczyk Winterhalter

☙

As a twelve-year-old seventh-grader, she survived a fall from a second-floor window instead of becoming one of ten fatalities in Room 208. Today she works as a paralegal and lives in Berkley, Michigan, where she and her retired husband, Tom, volunteer their services to help young adults recovering from drug and alcohol addictions.

My memories today are still pretty vivid. I imagine they are for a lot of the kids who were there. Sister Mary St. Canice was my teacher. We were in the first room by the back stairway, where the fire came up. Sister was talking about homework for a history test, and there was groaning and moaning about that. The first thing I recall was the rattling of the doors. It was unusual, and we started joking about it—that all the ghosts were trying to come in from the hallway. Then we started smelling smoke. I remember Sister saying, "Don't worry, that's probably just the furnace backing up." It seemed like in no time at all we started seeing smoke pouring in from the transoms above the doors. Sister told us just to sit down and try to be as calm as possible. But the smoke started coming in pretty fast, and from the smell of it we knew it was more than just a backup of the furnace.

Then, things happened very quickly. I remember flames licking over the top of the door and at the ceiling in the front of the room. My desk was closer to the windows, and I was watching as some of the kids tried to leave through the rear door. When they opened it, the smoke made it impossible to get out. So they slammed the door shut. Somebody started yelling, "Get to the windows! Get to the windows!" I remember seeing my girlfriend, Irene Mordarski, trying to climb up on the radiator and the fire getting to her. A lot of kids went to the windows toward the back of the room. I went to a window at the front, and I remember kids piling on top of me, struggling to breathe. It was just pandemonium. The globe lights, they were low-hanging lights, and I recall hearing them exploding from the intense heat. We wanted to get out, but there were no ladders. With the kids piled all over me, I really couldn't feel the heat until they moved toward the back of the room. I stayed there at the front window. I was kind of paralyzed, afraid to move. Sister Canice came up behind me and told me to get up on the windowsill. I was sitting on the ledge, and she said, "You gotta jump. You gotta get out of here." And I said, "No, I can't jump. I can't jump." Then she pushed me. She pushed me out.

I landed on that little slanting roof that covered an entrance to the basement chapel. I was fortunate to land there, otherwise I would have broken my back if I had hit the ground. I landed on the lower part of my back, and I've always had trouble with it since. I was lying on that little roof, and some neighborhood men came running over and helped me off. They carried me to the candy store. That's where they were taking some of the kids. The firemen had just started to arrive. I had lost my shoes and didn't have a coat. I was in my stocking feet, wearing a navy blue, jumper-style uniform and blouse. I was in the store until I was taken away by ambulance.

Fortunately I had no broken bones, but I lost probably several inches of hair from the fire and had burns on the back of my neck and the backs of my arms. But it was nothing serious. I am grateful to Sister Canice, because if it wasn't for her I wouldn't have gone out that window. I remember thinking to myself, a good, little Catholic girl, you know, that I had been to church on Sunday, received Holy Communion, and that I was ready to die and knew I'd go straight to heaven.

I don't know how long I waited before being put in the ambulance. Time was irrelevant. Everything was surreal. I don't even remember how they carried me out of the store.

We lived on Ferdinand Street, about six blocks from the school. After the fire I think I went to John Hay public school. I'm not sure. It's like I dissociated myself from a lot of what happened to me after that. I had a phobia of going into buildings. I had a phobia about getting into a place where I couldn't escape quickly. I remember going to one of those schools after OLA, sitting in a classroom, and the teachers, the nuns, in their great insensitivity, had us clipping out newspaper articles about the fire, and I just broke down.

I think about the school fire all the time. Every December is kind of a melancholy time for me. There have been people who have gotten together for fund-raisers and reunions, and I've contacted them on and off. But every time I get closer to it, the more pain I experience. I lost my teacher. She and I were somewhat close. I remember admiring her and wanting to be a nun too. I watched her so closely. My best friend, Christina Vitacco, died in the fire. A couple of other kids who were friends of mine died in my classroom. Christina's parents had a real hard time with her death. A couple of neighbors, the Chiappettas, lived right across the street from me. There were two Chiappettas who went to Our Lady of the Angels. The daughter, Joan Anne, died in the fire. She and I used to play in the street. There was . . . just so much pain and loss in it. There was never any real closure. There were no therapists running around to help you deal with the loss issues. There were no counselors around to help me with the question of why my friends died and I didn't.

It's like a catharsis to talk about our experiences in the fire rather than try to keep it all inside. We weren't taught that when we were younger. We felt we had to "grin and bear it, forget it, it's part of the past, don't talk about it any more." But that's not how a human being works. We have memories and we need to deal with the conflict, with the pain, and we need to heal it, talk about it. I understand now why therapists and counselors flock to areas where there are disasters or tragedies, especially when they involve young people who do not have enough experience with life to work through it. When we're young we need guidance, we need that input, that comfort. Not having help in getting through that ordeal damaged a lot of us. We had to search out answers on our own. And I think most of us did. I know I went to counseling for several years. My lifestyle was not only a product of what happened to me at the fire, it was also the result of what happened at home and the kind of family life I had. I experienced several traumas in my life, and the fire was one of the big ones. But you have to have the attitude that life is a blessing and is sacred regardless of what happens to you. When a door closes, God always opens a window for us.

My father's name was Anthony, my mother's name was Doris. I have a stepbrother John, who was born in America. I was born in Goettingen, Germany. My mom was born in the Ukraine, and my dad was Polish. We came to the United States in about 1951. My parents separated when we came to America, and my mother remarried.

Sister Canice, of course, was my favorite teacher at Our Lady of the Angels. I liked Sister Seraphica and the lay teacher, Miss [Dorothy] Coughlan. Sister Seraphica and my mother got along very well. My mother talked to the nuns a lot for advice. She felt comfortable with them. We had a rough family life. There were a lot of problems at home. The nuns gave my mother spiritual guidance at that time.

The school fire, I believe, increased our sensitivity to other people's problems. It gave us an understanding of the hardships and traumas people in other places in the world go through, what they're feeling or how difficult their recovery might be. It expanded our empathy for others. If I had to do it all over again, of course, I'd wish it had never happened. It was something you wouldn't want to happen to anybody. But it did. It helped improve the safety of schools in Chicago and the state, and had the same sort of effect nationwide. So some benefit came from the tragedy. The benefit that came to me was that it made me want to help other people.

All these years later, I still feel it was like an angel carrying me out of that building and getting me down on that roof. Other kids I knew who survived broke their ankles and legs, and Irene [Mordarski] shattered her hip. I was extremely fortunate. It took me a long time to realize that perhaps God had more work for me to do, and He wanted to keep me around for that. As I said, life is a blessing, every day is important, and you live the right way the best you can. That's what my husband and I do today. We work in our community, we work with people who are recovering from addictions. We get together usually twice a week with young adults, some of them seventeen or eighteen years old, who are recovering from drugs or alcohol. Maybe my desire to help others dates back to my young days at Our Lady of the Angels when I needed a great deal of help myself.

John Raymond

❧

He has spent much of his working life as an electrician and admits to some concern over an incipient arthritic condition in his right hip. He landed on it when he leaped from his classroom window during the fire. He and his wife live in Mount Prospect, Illinois, and have two sons and one grandson. He speaks sympathetically of his late father, the parish's overburdened janitor who suffered cruel allegations that he neglected to keep the school clean. He says his dad "helped save a lot of kids in one room, but he never really got over what happened that day."

Our family lived at 1008 North Hamlin, down the street from the church. My dad [James] was the janitor for all the parish buildings. That afternoon three of my brothers, my sister, and myself were attending Our Lady of the Angels. Bob was excused from Room 211 to help in the clothing drive. Tom was in Room 201. Mary Kay was in fourth grade, and Marty was in kindergarten in a building that was not involved in the fire. I was in fifth grade, Room 212. We were a faith-based family, and we thanked our lucky stars that we all got out because there was so much grief around us. Within half a block from where we lived, there were three kids who passed away.

We lived so close to the school that I used to go with my father a lot of times at night when he fired up the furnace in cold weather so the school would be warm the next morning. He'd usually be over there again at five in the morning to fire the furnace up once more. Then he'd come back home for breakfast. He was never the same, of course, after the school fire. He wasn't a big talker, but he just withdrew into a shell. Occasionally I talked to my mother about the fire. I remember a couple of years later we were going to one of those card-bunco parties. We were walking to a rented hall with a couple of women in the neighborhood. I don't know why I was going, but it was a parish thing. The women were talking about the fire, and my mother said, "I can't believe that God knew when that building was built it would be torn down for that reason." She wondered why it happened. My mother graduated from OLA in 1928. She gave me the lowdown on the whole neighborhood and on the early days of the parish.

After the fire I had been in the hospital, and I got home that following weekend. I had bruised my right hip pretty badly when I hit the ground after jumping from my classroom window. Everybody was anxious to get back together. I guess it was because we had survived. We were asked to gather in the church basement, and the sadness really started to hit then, when all the kids we knew weren't around any more. It sort of shocked me. There were quite a few of my close friends who didn't make it.

We then took up classes again at Our Lady Help of Christians, where they had to prepare the upper floors for us. We were there for maybe six weeks. From there we went to Orr public school. I'd walk a good six blocks to Orr, where they had a forced-air heating system. Probably the first fall we were there—you know the smell you get when you turn on the furnace the first time after it's been off for a while? That was the smell we got while we were in class. Everybody started to get nervous. And the nun, said "No, no, don't worry. Sit, sit." And everybody was like, "We're outta here." We weren't going to stay. We weren't going to listen to anybody. I was nervous myself. I remember one of the girls, she was a little thing. She was frightened, and I had to carry her down the stairs. We all filed out of the school. I remember seeing the school's engineer. He was a big, black man, weighed maybe 250 pounds. His name was Prendergast. He talked to us, explained what was going on and that everything was okay. Then we all went back in. From that day forward Mr. Prendergast was there every morning, greeting us as we went into the school. He gave us a good feeling. He was a nice man. He kept reassuring us that the school was safe.

I can tell you from my own experience that on the day of the fire, John Mele [one of the fatalities in Room 212] was sitting in front of me. Sebastian Rivan, a big Italian kid, he was sitting in the first row, last seat, and when he opened that back door the smoke poured in like you wouldn't believe. It was so black, that smoke. We never moved. Sister Mary Clare dashed down the aisle and slammed the door. I know there were others in my class who never moved, because when Sister Mary Clare said open the windows, kids who sat in the row near the windows opened them. That probably brought in more smoke. Shortly after that she said go to the windows. You're talking about fifty-some kids stampeding to the windows. I just sat there. My desk was in the middle of the room. I must have been in shock. I often wondered how I ended up on the floor. I don't know this for sure, but I think John Mele had passed out already and was lying on the floor. He hadn't moved. He had this white shirt on, and pretty soon it wasn't white any more. I got out of my desk and onto the floor. I realize now that I probably stumbled over John.

I've often thought that if we had gone out that back door, held each other's hands, and worked our way to the front stairs, which weren't that far, maybe most of us would've gotten out. Sister Mary Clare was twenty-seven years old. She had the responsibility of taking care of all these kids, and at the same time she had to follow the strict rules they had then, so we shouldn't make a judgment against her. Her decision was a tough one. We were well enveloped in smoke when the fire alarm went off, but we did have that moment where we could've gone out that door. I don't know if every kid would've been able to do that, though.

I crawled over to a window in the front of the room, and that's where I jumped. It was not a courageous thing—I was about to pass out. When I got to the front of the room, I remember I was by the teacher's desk, and that's when I heard the kids screaming—some of them were calling for Sister but most of them were calling for their mothers. I thought I was in a nightmare. I was getting delusional. What got me going was when I looked up at the lights, I could barely see them. I turned toward the door for some reason and felt the heat. At that point the air at the bottom of the floor was getting hot. It started to affect my lungs to such a degree I was ready to pass out. That's when I went to the window, pushed my way through, and dove out. I didn't stand on the window ledge, I just dove out for my life. It was a tough thing to do, but when I think about it now, it was what I had to do.

The surface below was hard gravel. I landed on my right hip. I never went to the doctor after that. Today you'd probably be going to the doctor every other week after getting hurt like that. I was limping around for a couple of months. I'm starting to feel aftereffects of that fall now, with some arthritis in my hip. But I was very fortunate. Probably because I was skinny, I didn't break anything.

One time when I was young, some fellow workers started talking about the fire and how it started. They didn't know I had been there. These were older guys, maybe in their forties and fifties. I'm like twenty-two and sort of in the background. One guy says, "Didn't the janitor do it?" That's when I had to pipe up. "No, the janitor didn't do it," I said. "The janitor was my father." They asked me, "Were you there?" And I said, "Yes." I had to set them straight.

We used to run into that sort of thing. My brother Bob said it happened to him once in a bar, where some guy blamed our father for the fire. Bob and my brother Tom were older than me, and we never talked much about the fire. Except I remember Bob saying he was mad that he had to leave his eighth-grade classroom to help on the clothing drive because jobs like that usually meant you had to stay around after school hours, when everybody else had gone home.

I figure what happened to me at the fire has held me back. For the most part I haven't gone through a single day when I haven't thought about it. There's always been something that reminded me of it . . . a red brick building like OLA, or any old public school. One year I was asked to talk to some kids about my experience in surviving the fire. This was at a school in Steger, Illinois, for mentally challenged kids, seventh-graders. They had been on a fire drill, had been goofing around, and the teacher was angry with them for doing that. She had chewed them out and told them the story about the Our Lady of the Angels fire. She brought the book *To Sleep with the Angels* to class and started reading a few pages a day to them. Two or three of the kids actually read the book. Their parents were shocked. They were saying the kids had "never read a book in their lives." I talked to the kids for about two hours, and they asked direct questions. On December 1 that year those kids set off ninety-five balloons with the name of a victim on each balloon. I have talked on the phone and in person to many other students who were doing papers on the school fire. It's amazing the interest in it. At another school over in Logan Square, where the students were almost all Hispanic, they asked me to come. And I went. It was in the auditorium where they had charts and stuff about the fire. It was almost eerie. These kids sat and listened intently during my entire talk. It was a good thing, because kids are so desensitized today.

My dad died in 1979; he was sixty-five. He had cancer and had gone through radical surgery. My mother lived to eighty-nine; she died a few years ago. Monsignor Cussen and my dad were pretty good buddies. Both of them never got over the fire. Another one who was deeply affected was Jimmy Erbstoesser. He was in my room. When I jumped, I think he called for me. He jumped too, and broke both ankles and I believe his right arm. We both crawled away and wound up sitting along the wall of the candy store on the other side of the alley. We were kind of buddies. We were watching what was going on, and the woman from the candy store threw something like a curtain over us.

Next thing I know, Jimmy is just out of it. You could see the stare in his eyes.

Afterward we both went to Orr, and that summer the American Legion gave us all trips to a camp up in Coloma, Michigan. We went up there for two weeks. When we got back to the train station in Chicago, Jimmy's mother was there. They had moved in the meantime to the South Side, to 79th and Kostner. When I was only eleven, I used to go out on a bus by myself and see Jimmy at their place and stay for a night. Jimmy ran away when he was in the eighth grade. And, I don't know, he just never . . . he was just kinda messed up. He took off and his mother used to call me and ask, "Has he come by you?" And I'd say, "No, he hasn't been here." They hired an investigator and found him up in Wisconsin, working on a farm. He used to love horses. Then he ran away again. He was gone until he was twenty-two, twenty-three years old, out in Arizona, I think, and then he ended up in Texas. He married a Mormon girl and had five kids. I haven't gotten a card from him, but recently somebody told me he's still in Georgetown, Texas. Without question the school fire affected him pretty badly. He and I used to talk about it all the time.

I think there's something to be said about going to a Catholic grammar school. You keep those ties. I have friends right now that I have not lost contact with since our school days. I see them all the time. It's a wonderful feeling to have friends for over fifty years. It's just unbelievable, it really is.

William Edington

🌿

*He and his wife, Pearl, live in Luther Village, a retirement
complex in Arlington Heights, Illinois. Their eldest son,
Bill, an eighth-grader, suffered severe burns from flames
that raged in Room 211 and became the last fatality of Our
Lady of the Angels fire, dying on August 9, 1959. Another
son, Ron, and two daughters, Carol and Pat, were also
in attendance at the school on the day of the tragedy. A
sixth-grade student in Room 205, Ron exited safely from
the building. He later served twenty-six years in the navy
before reentering civilian life in 1995. His father retired as
an engineer with AT&T in 1984. The Edingtons have five
grandchildren.*

It was a hectic day, I'll tell you that. I'm eighty-five years
old, and the memories of what happened are still with
me. I was at work, but I didn't learn about the fire there. I
worked till four o'clock. I was out in Skokie at the Teletype
Corporation. I got in my car, drove south on the Edens
Expressway, and was going down Cicero Avenue with the
radio on. They broke in and said, "Our Lady of the Angels
School is on fire." It didn't hit me right away. You know

how you listen to the radio when you're driving and some guy is talking, you're not paying close attention. So I said to myself, "Holy mackerel, what did I hear?" In my mind, I wanted him to repeat it. And he did. And I went, "Oh, my God!" I had four kids in that school. So I went down Cicero Avenue doing about sixty miles an hour, hoping a police officer would stop me and help get me there in no time. But I didn't get an escort because I imagine there were a lot of police at the scene of the fire.

I proceeded down Cicero, and when I finally got to Division Street they had it barricaded. I got out of the car and said to the guy, "Move that barricade." And the guy says, "What are you, nuts?" I said, "Yeah, I'm nuts. I got four kids in that school." So he pulls the barricade aside and says, "Go!"

I headed home. We lived in a house at 922 North St. Louis. Everybody was worked up at home. Nobody had called me at work. I asked, "Okay, what's what?" They said, "Well, we heard about Ron, we heard about Pat, we heard about Carol." Pat and Carol had been taken to a neighbor's home. They took the kids in. It was cold. But we didn't hear from Bill. He was the kind who'd just say, "Here I am." I thought, "Oh, oh, he should be home by now telling us he was okay. He must be in trouble." So we had to wait, couldn't find out about Bill.

We finally got a call from the hospital, St. Anne's. They said Bill was there. My wife and I rushed to the hospital. We didn't see Bill right away, but we heard he was going into surgery. We talked to the doctor. He said he had worked on burns in the army, and he told us, "He won't live through the night." We waited and waited, stayed there, and finally the doctor came out again. He says, "Are you still here?"

We asked, "Is he still alive?" The doctor says, "Yes, I've got to go work on him." From then on, it was a little more than eight months that Bill lived. The doctor thought Bill was going to make it. He had more stitches in him than a suit of clothes, the doctor said. Bill went through hell, you know. He was burned over 87 percent of his body. And 63 percent was third degree.

The doctor kept him alive, that's all we knew. We didn't ask him any questions. He used to go into surgery and come out looking like he hadn't slept for a week. My wife and a friend of ours, Helen Reidy, agreed to give skin for Bill, who needed lots of grafts. My wife gave 220 square inches, and Helen Reidy, she gave 240. So Bill got 460 square inches of skin and it covered only his back. The doctor told the women that when he took off their skin, it would be like a burn. My wife and Helen had permanent scars from these donations.

In the hospital Bill was the first one to have that electric bed that went around in a circle. With it they could stand him up or lay him down. He was in a Stryker bed at first, a straight bed that you could turn around. He didn't like that bed, and I didn't either. It was tough for us to see him like that for roughly eight months with those burns. It finally got him. He got a bad batch of blood from a transfusion, that's what the doctor said. The doctor was wonderful. Never sent in a bill. He worked for nothing. Bill was the last to go. Another student, Valerie Thoma, died a few months before him.

When Bill was in his hospital bed, they had him face down and the nurses, interns, and his doctor were in the room. They were working on him, and I saw a puddle of water beneath his bed. He was crying. He was a good sport

73

about this. I said, "What's the matter, Bill?" He says, "Will you please tell 'em to leave me alone?" He had had enough. I told the doctor who said, "Okay."

And they all went out of the room. That was the beginning of the end for Bill. One night he called us on the phone and asked us to bring him some "slop aid" and pizza. We said, "Sure." When we got there they had him propped up in his bed. We gave him the pizza and "slop aid"—that's what he called Kool-Aid. He took a bite of the pizza. His appetite was gone. He had the Kool-Aid, and he said to us, "You mind if I go to sleep?" We said, "No, go ahead, Bill." And that's the last time we talked to him. The following night he went into a coma and passed away. Bill was a little fighter. I told the doctor I wished I could take his place.

Bill was a very athletic, wiry boy. We asked him, "How come you stayed so long in your school room?" He could've jumped. If he broke a leg, okay. He told us, "I stayed because the little guys couldn't get any air at the windows, so I would pull the big guys away and let the little guys get up by the windows." As a result, he stayed too long. He also told us that the fire was coming out of the cracks of the blackboard before he got out. You know, Nancy Smid lost her life [in Room 212]. On Sunday I had taken the kids home from church, and little Nancy was one of them. When she got out of the car, she looked up at me in the driver's seat and said, "Thank you, Mr. Edington." I said, "That's okay, Nancy." And that was the last time I talked to her.

I think a lot about the loss many parents suffered. When you lose a sibling, that's a bummer. It remains with you for the rest of your life. The memories stay with you. I can even remember Bill's boyfriend saying that Bill was the fastest guy in the neighborhood. He used to run in races with sixteen-year-olds, and he'd beat 'em. I recall one time he was swimming in the Fox River. It was at a picnic, and they were going to have a race for kids. He wasn't fourteen yet, but he got into the race with sixteen-year-olds, and he missed by a foot beating them all. He played Little League baseball. One time he hit a ball, came around second base, and when he got to third base the guy was blocking the bag. Bill went around him and got tagged out. I got ahold of him on the sideline. I said, "Bill, when somebody blocks the bag, baseball is baseball, you've got to go into him." He says to me, "Look, Dad, I want to play ball. I don't want to hurt anybody." I said, "Okay," and I put my tail between my legs and left.

In school Bill was an altar boy and a patrol boy. All the neighborhood kids liked him. When he was in the hospital, they took turns taking his paper route. My wife was a redhead, and our daughter, Carol, was a redhead, and Bill was a little bit lighter than she was. We buried Bill at St. Joseph's Cemetery at Belmont and Cumberland. They said that before he was waked, the undertakers looked at his body and got down on their knees and were praying.

I recall an incident at St. Anne's when I was there with Bill. Next door there were two heart-attack victims, and the door to their room was open. I'm not overly religious, but I'm Catholic. While I'm in the room, Bill says, "Give me the rosary." And I said, "Where is it?" He says, "Hurry up." I asked him why. But he just says again, "Hurry up. Gimme the rosary." So I gave him the rosary and he started to pray. I looked in the room next to him. The guys in the room had heard him and got out of their beds and knelt down to pray for him. The nun also rushed in and was kneeling and praying. What Bill saw, I don't know. Maybe he had a premonition of his death. But he says to his nurse, Miss Dalton, "What's heaven like?" And she says, "Oh, it's beautiful." He says, "I'm going to find out."

I'll tell you how the school fire still affects us. I learned about a website on the fire. I pulled it up on my computer and saw that it had pictures. When my wife and I looked at them, tears just rolled from our eyes. That's part of the aftermath of the fire. You never forget. We remember how we suffered. You cannot forget that. Anyone who says they can forget that, they're lying. Even though we had three wonderful kids, you remember the one who died. What do you call that? A stigma? When they play that song "Moonlight and Roses," I don't know why that reminds me of Bill, but it does. I just hope nothing like that school fire ever happens again. It takes something out of you. But you have to go on with your life. You can't take it out on people because you lose somebody. You can be alone with each other and think about it, but you can't go around with a pout on your face.

I do know that after the fire I became very safety conscious. I bought a fire extinguisher for the house. I even fashioned a long, heavy rope and put knots in it, so the kids could use it to get out of an upper bedroom if the house caught fire. I told 'em, "If fire breaks out downstairs, tie this rope around a bedstead and use it to go out the window. Don't go downstairs for your mother and me. Just go." I even put a baseball bat in the bedroom. I said to them, "Use the bat to break the window if you can't get it open."

I'll end my story with this: When I got home on that afternoon of the fire, the car kept rolling to the curb while I jumped out and went in the house. They told me Bill was missing. I went to the school. I saw the firemen coming down the ladders, shaking their heads. They evidently hated to go up there. At the hospital later I asked my Bill, "What were the firemen doing?" He said, "The first firemen were crying because they couldn't get to us. They were crying down there."

When you look at the whole situation, I think the grownups failed the kids. If some of the people who were there early could've brought out mattresses, they might've been able to cushion the kids' falls. And they had that iron fence blocking the courtyard. I imagine some truck could've knocked it down. But nobody thought. I guess under that sort of pressure, you really don't think.

When Bill was rescued by the fireman, he said he was almost unconscious, and he felt cold hands grabbing him. That's all he remembered then. The doctor said nobody lives with the degree of burns he had. When Bill had lived for about eight months, the doctor [Dr. Bill Dvonch] went on vacation. When he came back, it was bad, and he said, "I never would have gone on vacation if I thought this was going to happen." They would stand Bill up on that bed and put paper on the floor because his body fluids would run out. He had terrific burns. I have no regrets about his hospital care. The nurses and doctors were wonderful. They did one heck of a job. They did the best they could at that time. But in the end Bill went to sleep with the angels.

Charlene Campanale Jancik

✿

In 2003 she became president of the newly reconstituted Friends of OLA, and on February 9 that year she recounted her painful survival of the school fire during which she suffered a broken back and pelvis in a desperate leap from a second-floor window. In October 2003 she was hospitalized with a brain aneurysm, underwent surgery, fell into a coma, and died at age fifty-four on November 30. Her passing was a crushing loss for her family and her many friends from Our Lady of the Angels. She left her husband, Wayne, and son, Matthew. The message she wrote less than ten months before her death follows and serves as a poignant reminder of her courage and her dedication to a school she loved.

I was in Grade 4 in Room 210 with Sister Seraphica at the time of the fire. We all smelled smoke and kept interrupting the lesson to tell the nun, but she dismissed it as "burning leaves," which was legally permitted at that time. The smoke kept getting stronger. Within two minutes of our first noticing the smell, thick, dark, intense smoke began pouring in over the transom. We all gasped, and Sister ordered us to stand up and pray the rosary. She went to the back door of the classroom and pushed it open.

The fire gases blew this door open very hard, pushing Sister against the back wall. We all lost control at that point, stopped praying, and ran for the windows. The nun ordered the bigger boys in our room to lower the upper windows. I saw her waving her hands and trying to hush us down. Everyone was screaming, crying, and pounding on the windowsills, asking for help, crying for their mommies.

The people on the pavement below included mothers and the grocery store owner from across the alley we were facing. They were telling us not to jump, that the firemen would be coming soon. My best friend, Janet Gasetler, came up to me. She was crying, and her skin was full of red and white blotches. She screamed to me, "Charlene, Charlene, I'm so scared!" I don't remember saying anything myself. I don't remember crying or screaming. I was totally numb. I felt like I was in a nightmare, that I was disconnecting with reality. I kept remembering the commercials over the summer that said, "If you're drowning, don't panic," and I kept saying that to myself.

I could see Room 212 on the left side of me, with fifth-graders who were just as hysterical as we were. I could also see Room 208, with seventh-graders, on the right side of our room, and they were also hysterical. In other rooms some boys were now jumping out of the windows. I remember thinking that I wished I were older and bigger, but I wasn't. I saw many of the adults on the pavement below, kneeling, praying, crying and screaming. The pavement looked like a war zone to me, with many of the jumpers covered with blood. I noticed that the ones who jumped were either lying very still on the pavement or were propped up against the wall of the candy store across the alley, with blood streaming down their faces, and that some of them were talking to one another. This gave me the idea that you could jump and be okay. I also spotted one of my former neighbors, Johanna Uting, lying face down on the pavement, but as she turned around I could see that her leg was split open and covered with blood. As I looked down at her, I knew that if she could do it, I could do it too.

I took off my glasses and threw them down on the pavement below. I wished that I could be where my glasses were. I was now choking and coughing from the smoke, and so was everyone else. I was having trouble breathing, so I felt I had to get out. I started to climb up on the windowsill, but each time I tried, a group of boys behind me grabbed my blouse and legs and pulled me back, telling me not to jump, that I'd hurt myself. Then I remember the firemen coming, and they put up ladders in the other classroom windows first. Everyone in our room was pounding and screaming for them to put the ladders in our windows. When we first saw the firemen pulling up, everyone cheered because we assumed they would rescue all of us.

Finally I got up on the windowsill, kicked backward, and wiggled away from the boys who were trying to stop me. I had to fight to get out of that window. I climbed up on the outer ledge of the window, and I remember standing straight up. At that point I either passed out or jumped. I went into shock.

My grandmother came to get me and kept screaming my name. She said there were so many bodies on the ground, she couldn't see mine. As she called my name, I answered her with "Grandma, I'm here!" I do not remember saying that because I was still in shock. I started to regain consciousness when my grandmother and two young women were carrying me to her car and laying me in the back seat. I remember the two women crying and saying, "The poor dear." My grandmother was crying too, swearing and praying in Polish. She drove to our house and then went into the grocery store—Sally's, at Thomas and Springfield, next door. She left the back door of the car open and ran to phone my mom at work. The owners of the store, Stanley and Sally, and the customers came to the back door of the car and peered in at me. When my grandmother came out, Stanley told her not to drive as she was too hysterical, and he got in the car to drive. She was in the front seat with him. Stanley drove very fast and was pulled over by a policeman who scolded him for driving too fast. My grandmother and Stanley screamed that there had been a school fire and that there would be others rushing to hospitals. The policeman then put on his siren and escorted us to the hospital.

At the hospital they pulled a stretcher up to the car, and the nurses and orderlies started to pull me out of the back seat. This is when I had my first feeling of huge pain. I screamed as they got me on the stretcher and rushed me into the x-ray room where they started to cut off my uniform with scissors. My mother came in, and when the doctor asked me where I felt pain, I screamed, "My back!" My mother got hysterical at this point, and they escorted her from the room. After x-rays they wheeled me up to a room. I was not to eat or drink, but my throat was so dry and rough that I kept begging for water. My aunt was there, and they let her pat my lips with a wet cloth. I kept trying to suck the water out. I was told I was on the critical list, and a priest came in and gave me last rites.

I was not allowed to turn on my side and was told to lie completely on my back, which was very uncomfortable without any pillow. I had to remain that way for three months, with head traction and weights pulling my head upward and with a towel rolled under my spine. During that time I also had lots of problems with my intestinal system, because I had been lying down constantly. Since I was at Norwegian American Hospital and not in one of the other hospitals where most of the fire victims were taken, I did not get all the gifts and cards that other students received. After my mother called the *Chicago Sun-Times*, they published two articles about me. I then got seven thousand cards and gifts from around the world the first week alone. The second week I got four thousand cards and gifts, and they kept coming. Eventually it took us two years to read and sort through them all.

I remember one woman named Mary Martin, who lived in Kalamazoo, Michigan, actually sent me a present every day! Also, Jim Moran, the Courtesy Motors man who had a car business in our neighborhood, invited all the fire victims to a gathering where the Cisco Kid was the big attraction and we had box lunches of fried chicken. A member of the Shriners then carried me up a flight of stairs to see the circus. He also offered to buy us anything we wanted. My grandmother wanted me to ask for a stereo unit, which was expensive in those days, so I did.

At the end of February 1959 I left the hospital with a body cast that covered my entire torso. At home I still had to lie in bed most of the time or sit with the traction device strapped on. One of the lay teachers from school was sent to tutor me. Later a group of us, including Teresa Whittaker and Frank Della, came to my home for summer-school lessons. I remember seeing how badly burned they were, but since I was the only one not walking, they had to come to my home. That summer we were linked to another small group that was being tutored by another teacher, Miss Coughlan. My teacher was Miss Tristano. All the fire victims were invited to a special summer overnight camp, but I could not go because I couldn't walk, so my cousin went for me. I remember crying about that one.

I continued to have nightmares about the fire, and for the next four years I would wake up drenched in sweat. I had to have my pajamas changed in the middle of the night. I had one episode where I saw a shadow move across our front door and started screaming that it was a fire. My mother got me in the car and drove me to a doctor who never even saw me and prescribed tranquilizers. I was moved to my grandmother's apartment, on the first floor of our two-flat. I felt better on the first floor. I figured I would not have to jump so far if anything were to happen.

After seven months of the body cast and wheelchair, I was put in a torso brace that allowed me to do some walking. I still could not get up stairs and had to go to Immaculate Conception School because it had an elevator. Emotionally I still could not handle going into schools, and my mother had to sit in the school office every day to help me make that transition. Eventually she would leave the school for short breaks, and then finally she stopped coming. During our first fire drill at the school, one little boy behind me kept teasing me and telling me it was a real fire. I got hysterical until the nun stopped him and comforted me.

I returned to Our Lady of the Angels after the new school was built. I was in sixth grade. Every fire drill made my heart beat fast; I felt a sense of panic each time. It took me many years to be able to talk about the fire. After meeting my husband at age nineteen, I did not tell him about the fire until three years later. Now I feel secure enough to talk about it. Eventually I became a teacher in special education and work in a school every day.

Lois Wille

💮

*During a distinguished career in journalism she won
two Pulitzer Prizes, in 1963 for a series of articles on
government's failure to provide birth-control data and
services to indigent women, and in 1989 for editorial
writing. She served as the editorial page editor for three of
the city's major newspapers, the* Chicago Daily News, *the*
Sun-Times, *and the* Tribune, *retiring in 1991. In 1972 she
wrote* Forever Open, Free and Clear, *a highly acclaimed
book dealing with the long struggle to protect the city's
lakefront. She grew up in Arlington Heights, Illinois, and
today lives in Chicago with her husband, Wayne. She says
she'll never forget her visit on the night of the fire with the
parents whose adopted daughter died in Room 212.*

The day started with me filling in at the city desk for Margaret Whitesides as the phone girl. That's what they used to
call Margaret. The *Daily News* was such a sexist-structured
organization then that when Margaret went on vacation
only another female could fill in for her. Since I was the
only female on general assignment, that was my job. I was
a fairly new reporter then. I had joined the paper in 1957.

I remember fire alarms came in all the time. Bells would ring. And Bill Mooney, our rewrite man, was so experienced with that procedure and with every corner of the city that he knew what a series of rings indicated. When the alarm sounded, he shouted, "That's a school box!" He quickly went to a file that decodes the bell signals, and got the address and name of the school: Our Lady of the Angels.

I spent the rest of the afternoon taking phone calls from worried parents seeking information, or passing phone calls from the reporters on to the sitting city editor, John Justin Smith. I did that until about 5:30 or so, the time Margaret would normally go home. I must have spent three hours passing phone messages back and forth in those days before BlackBerries. They knew then that we'd need more people to cover the various aspects of the story, reporters who could go to the hospitals, the morgue, and even homes of parents whose children were attending the school.

About that time another reporter, Bob Schultz, and I were given assignments by assistant city editor Jim McCartney to go out to the school. We went there with a photographer who drove us to the school as a starting point. I was asked to look for parents of a dead child. It was a horrible assignment under any circumstances, especially since I was fairly new then. I wasn't sure what to do. With a photographer, we made the rounds of the hospitals. Bob may have found his family at one of the hospitals. I can still remember how horrible I felt, asking grieving parents if they had found out how their child was. Everybody was nervous and crying. I didn't want to say, "Is your child close to death?" I really didn't want to do that any more. At St. Anne's Hospital I finally met this couple—I knew they had a little girl who had died there. I asked them if I could talk to them.

I expected them to command me to get away from them. Instead they asked me if I'd go home with them. It was just the most extraordinary experience. I thought they wouldn't want to talk, but they wanted to do nothing *but* talk about their little girl. It was heartbreaking. I traveled with them to their home, and the photographer followed.

When we got to their house they showed me pictures of their daughter and a scrapbook and her first Communion dress. It was terribly hard for all of us. Something drove them just to want to talk about her. Maybe all they could think of at that moment was wanting other people to know her, and to keep her alive that way. I spent a number of hours with them, and then went back to the office with the photographer. When I got back to my desk, other reporters were drifting in. It must have been 2 or 3 a.m. It was getting close to deadline, and my mind was just a blank. I don't even remember writing the story about the girl, but I know I must have finished it before 7 a.m. I had worked around the o'clock, and it must have been nine or ten in the morning before I left.

It was the first story of such tragic proportions that I had worked on. It was a traumatic experience. When I started at the *Daily News* in the building on Madison Street, I was in what they called the women's section until 1958. At that time it was the newspaper's policy to have only two women in the newsroom. Helen Fleming, who covered education, was one, and the other female had quit to enlist in the Marines, so I got her job as a general assignment reporter. But I did mainly feature stories, nothing like the school fire. My first assignment was to fly with the Navy Blue Angels, and the city editor had me brush the teeth of a hippopotamus at Brookfield Zoo with a huge scrubbing brush, and play billiards with Willie Mosconi. Things like that. Not anything significant like writing about the grief caused by the school fire.

I think of the fire quite often. Every anniversary, for sure. It still is so much a part of the city today. Wayne and I live in a huge, heavy-timbered building on the near South Side that was once a cold-storage warehouse. The developers who converted the place into residential condos had to have sprinklers installed because Chicago's building code was heavily influenced by the school fire.

For me, visiting with those parents who lost their girl remains unforgettable. In recent years there's been a lot of talk of reporters barging in on people during moments like that and how awful it is, putting a microphone in the face of someone who has been through a tragedy and asking, "How do you feel?" Every time I read somebody's criticism of how reporters behave, I think of that night all over again, and how I felt asking Margaret's parents if I could talk with them. I was so embarrassed and ashamed that I had to do that to them. But they opened up to me. They had to do it for their little girl.

What follows is Lois Wille's article that appeared in the Chicago Daily News *on Tuesday, December 2, 1958:*

Her name was Margaret Kucan. She was one of those who died. She was ten and had auburn hair and her father says her eyes sparkled like jewels. She was going to be a nun or maybe a zookeeper. She wasn't sure yet, but she had so much time to make up her mind.

This is the story of Margaret, the kind of girl she was, perhaps the same kind of girl as so many others who died.

And, it's the story of how one family learned the awful news.

Margaret's father, Slavko, thirty-seven, is a barber who came from Yugoslavia in 1930. He and his wife Yola, thirty-six, live in a spotless apartment at 3814 Chicago Avenue. That's just one block away from Our Lady of the Angels School.

Slavko Kucan, short and husky and black-haired, wanted to talk about his little girl Monday night. His eyes were red and he clutched a handkerchief in his fist, but he wasn't crying. Not any more. He spoke in soft, steady tones:

"Oh, such a good daughter. So good. A gentle girl, a sweet and quiet girl. She was everything we ever wanted. We adopted her from St. Vincent's Orphanage when she was just six weeks old—just a tiny, helpless baby. She was the child we longed for.

"There were so many things she loved," her father said. "Animals and little children and ice skating. I had promised to take her ice skating next Sunday. Sometimes, after school, she would play nun. She fixed a headpiece, like nuns wear, and put on her rosaries. She'd play school. Johnny, her adopted brother, was her star pupil. He doesn't know his sister is dead. . . ."

Margaret's proudest hour came just eight days before she died. She was confirmed at Our Lady of the Angels Church on Sunday, November 23. "She was so excited," said her cousin, Judy Vavro, eleven, "that she got sick for two days and almost couldn't go." Judy and her mother Lydia, and fifteen other uncles and aunts, cousins and neighbors gathered in the Kucan home Monday night. They sat silently in the living room and around the dining room table. Grandma and grandpa, Mr. and Mrs. John Kucan of 1417 N. Keeler, were there, too. Two were missing: Margaret's mother, in bed under a doctor's care, and little Johnny. He was next door with a neighbor, asleep.

In the kitchen, Margaret's dog whimpered and scratched at the door. "At first, I thought I'd give him away," Margaret's father said. "She loved him so much, I thought it would hurt to look at him. But, I changed my mind. I'll keep him and love him till he dies."

Slavko Kucan was one of the first on the scene of the fire. He was in his barbershop when someone yelled that the school was burning. "I told my customers to wait and I ran over there," he said. "I saw smoke coming from the corner where Margaret's room was. I went up a ladder, but I just couldn't see her. I just didn't see her any place. I pulled other kids down. They were bloody and burned and didn't know what was happening. But, no Margaret, no Margaret."

About an hour later, Slavko went home to put on dry clothes and comfort his wife. He was there when the phone rang. "It was from my sister-in-law, Fern Kucan," he said. "She's a nurse at St. Anne's hospital. She said, 'I've got some news for you and it's bad, Slav . . . it's terribly bad . . .'"

Jean Hart

🌺

*A resident of Chicago's Northwest Side, she has been a
teacher in both grade schools and high schools for more
than forty years. She has frequently talked to her own
students and on invitation to other groups about her
experience in surviving the fire at Our Lady of the Angels.
She speaks warmly of her companion eighth-graders.
"Remember, we lived in a blue-collar neighborhood," she
says, "and we produced two doctors, half a dozen nurses,
and a ton of teachers, firemen, and police officers. I don't
think all of that came about by accident."*

I was sitting in the second or third desk from the front
of the room [209] because I'm short. My seat was in the
second row from the doors, near my friends, like Jimmy
Howard and Gloria Berg. One of the boys got up to open
the back door to get some fresh air because it started to
feel stuffy, and the smoke just billowed into the room. For
a couple of seconds, no one moved. The back door was shut
right away. Sister Davidis had us put some books at the bottom of the doors to block the smoke. I remember looking
up at the glass transoms over the doors and seeing the black

smoke up there. We all went over to the windows. Even though I sat in the front of the room, somehow I ended up at the back window.

We stuck our heads out the window and took a breath. Then we moved behind our friends who went in front of us so they could breathe in some air. We just kind of moved in a circle. Below our window was a little roof over stairs that led from a door in the annex of the school. A couple of the boys jumped onto that successfully, but when one of them jumped, his foot went through it. I remember that scared me a little bit. I was thinking I couldn't jump. I was a kid. I had just turned thirteen two weeks before. You don't know why you think certain things. I just thought it was too much to jump. I thought I'd kill myself if I hit the cement. About that time Rose Tortorice's dad came to a window in that U-shaped part of the building. Rose was in my room. He yelled to Rose to come to him. We got up on the windowsill. I was not the first one on the windowsill and not the last. Sister Davidis held my legs as I turned around. So now I was standing outside the window as Sister steadied me. I was okay with climbing. I had been a little bit of a tomboy as a younger kid, so I was able to jump up and grab the rain gutter. I sort of monkey-barred across to Rose's dad who pulled me in the annex window.

I remember Sister Davidis yelling to us when we were at the windows to space out so we wouldn't get jammed together. We were all eighth-graders. We probably weighed a hundred pounds each. I don't know whether she was that smart or that cool, but I'll tell you, she saved my life. After Rose's dad pulled me in, I was running down the stairs to get out on the Iowa Street side, and I ran right past Father Joe Ognibene who was running up. He asked me if I was okay, and I told him I was. He told me to go into the church, and I kept going. I went out the front door and into the church. A couple of minutes later my friend Gloria Berg came into the church and knelt down next to me, and she was crying. We were both flustered. They told us our parents would be looking for us and that it would be better if we went home. After we left the church, we did not go back around the corner to look at the school. They didn't want us to do that, and I'm glad we didn't. But I had seen kids jumping. I had seen kids in heavy smoke before I got out myself.

I was one little, only child, no brothers, no sisters. I lived at 4231 West Division Street, third-floor apartment. My father's name was Bud Hart—his real first name was Lawrence. My mother's name was Margaret. My dad was a sheet-metal worker. Gloria and I left the church together. She lived on Springfield Avenue, so we headed north on Hamlin to Division and walked west to Springfield. We went to her house and knocked on the back door. Her mother was on the phone. She looked out the back door and saw us. When she opened the door, she said, "What are you girls doing here?" Then she noticed our white blouses were all dark and that we had smoke under our noses and mouths. We pointed at the sky, at the smoke coming from the school, and she grabbed us both. She gave us something hot to drink and said to me, "I want to keep you here so I know you're safe, but your father is going to be looking for you." So she gave me Gloria's older sister's Sunday coat to wear home because it was cold. I walked the rest of the way home alone.

The news was then on the radio, and my dad heard it at work. He was working outside on a storefront, but they had a radio on. He dropped his tools, got in his car, and headed for OLA. My grandfather did the same kind of work, and he did exactly the same thing. My mother had been with the mother of Marne Hudson, another girl in my room. They had gone out to get their hair done and had just come home from the beauty shop. My mother stopped at the Certified grocery store at the corner of Keeler and Division. Marne's mother went upstairs to their apartment and heard about the fire on the radio. She ran back down the stairs and over to the grocery. She opened the door and yelled to my mother, "The school's on fire!" My mother left her grocery cart in the middle of the aisle and rode with Marne's mother in their car. They headed for the school but couldn't get any closer than a few blocks because of the traffic jam.

When my dad got to the building he knew just where to look, because a few days before there had been a parents' open-house night at the school where the parents visited their kids' classrooms. From what he saw, he knew it didn't look good. He asked some of the kids if they had seen me. One of them said he thought he saw me going away in an ambulance. So my dad headed back to his car and started down Division Street toward St. Anne's Hospital. But first he decided to check our house. When he came home, I thought I was going to spend the rest of my life sitting in my father's lap because he wasn't going to let me go. I was his little princess.

My dad was a wonderful guy with a heart of gold. He had spent World War II as a Marine in the Pacific. Although he would give you the shirt off his back, he was also tough as nails. He just instinctively knew what to do for me. I was always allowed to talk about the fire later. If I woke up in the middle of the night, I could go get dad and wake him up too, and talk about whatever was bothering me. My mother was more stoic, but my dad, he was in charge of the house.

When I first came home that afternoon, the phone started ringing off the hook. Aunts and uncles, grandparents, everyone calling to make sure I was okay. Everyone in the neighborhood was going through the same thing. I remember my dad saying, "Tomorrow your mother's going to take you to buy a new coat." He was kinda planning ahead. "We're going to take your uniform to the cleaners," he said, "and if we don't get the smoke out of it after a cleaning or two, we'll get you a new one."

Shortly thereafter we started going to Our Lady Help of Christians School. We went to OLA every morning and stood in our lines as we always did, waiting for the buses. We actually stood in front of the burned-out shell of our school, right on Avers Avenue. People couldn't believe they had many of us lined up right outside the burned building. I could still smell the smoke.

After Our Lady Help of Christians, I went to Orr public school. I remember they told us at Orr that we were going to have recess. Recess? We didn't know what the heck that was. We didn't have recess at OLA. We're going out to the playground in the middle of the day? My friend and I were put in charge of the second-grade girls at recess.

While I was at Orr, my friend Marne had ended up in the hospital. She was a tall girl, very slender. She had jumped from the fire and landed on her left side. She broke her left leg, her left arm, ribs on her left side, and her left jaw. She told me she never cried while she was in the hospital. She finally came back to school when we were at Orr. On maybe her second day back, there was some sort of a backup in the school's oil furnace and smoke started to billow in.

Well, we went into overdrive. They didn't have to ring an alarm, they didn't have to do anything to alert us. We ran out of our room. I went up four stairways to the little room the second-graders were in, and I grabbed the girls I was in charge of. We went out the stairs and out the building, and you could not have pulled us back into Orr that day with Clydesdales. Marne was so scared that she was home-schooled for the rest of eighth grade.

Orr was maybe two and a half blocks from my house. As I walked to school, sometimes when I was about half-way there I'd get sick to my stomach and go back home. I guess you'd call it post-traumatic stress. My dad took me to our family doctor, the same doctor who delivered me. He looked me over, made sure everything was okay, and he said, "This little girl has gone through something pretty tough, and if she's sick, let her come back home." He said to me, "When you come home sick, don't drink anything cold. Don't drink milk. Have some warm water or warm tea. If you think you can go back to school after lunch, then go ahead. If you can't, it's okay." My dad was fine with that. So I never got hassled about coming home, and most days I could make it to school. But if once in a while I couldn't, that was okay with my dad because he knew I wasn't lying to him for cutting school.

After graduating in 1959, I went to Siena High School. It was an all-girls school run by the Mercy nuns. I made new friends at Siena and kept the old friends from OLA. After four years there I went to St. Dominic College in St. Charles. I finished college in 1967 and started teaching, which I've done ever since.

Looking back on my life, I remember every day how lucky I am. I'm very tightly connected with my grade-school friends. We went through hell together. Jimmy Howard and I were always together. First of all, we were both short and, second, our last names were close alphabetically. So Jimmy always sat next to me or behind me in the classroom. We were partners for first Communion and for Confirmation.

Since the fire I've not been too worried about being up high. When I was younger I lived on the sixth floor of a condominium, and that didn't bother me. There *have* been things that trigger in me the thought of taking flight. One of them is the definite smell of smoke, an oily kind of smoke. It's never a problem for me to be in somebody's living room with a fireplace burning. Never. It's never a problem for me to go camping, for instance, and be near a fire for cooking. That's never bothered me. But there have been times when I've been teaching in a building, especially those that used to have oil boilers, where'd I'd get that kickback of oily smoke and I'd feel myself go into a cold sweat. I'd be thinking, "Get the kids out. Get out with them." I've had teachers that I've worked with say, "Are you okay? You look pale."

I've always felt I was three minutes away from having the serious injuries that Gerry Andreoli or Marne Hudson or Jimmy Howard suffered. I've also felt I was five minutes away from being dead. I know every day how lucky I am.

Ron Sarno

❦

Semi-retired after selling a restaurant furniture factory to his partner, he lives in Bloomingdale, Illinois, with his son. He survived without injury after jumping from Room 210, though his sister died in the same room and his older brother was a fatality in Room 211. Troubled with drug and alcohol addictions in his youth, he cleaned up his act and has been sober for more than twenty years.

My sister Joanne was in the same fourth-grade room with me. I was ten, and she was actually one year younger than me because I was put behind in third grade. I can remember that we were handing in test papers or something when all of a sudden I heard a girl screaming. I looked up and there was black smoke coming in through the transom above the door. Everybody stood up and looked at each other. The nun, Sister Seraphica, she went to the back door, opened it, and the smoke just started barreling in. She shut the back door and ran to the front of the room. She was trying to keep the kids calm. I look back on that situation and think, God, here's a room full of nine- and ten-year-olds, and it's this nun's job to try to keep them calm. When I hear people blaming the nuns for what happened, it upsets me. The nuns had such a burden on their shoulders that day.

But I can remember Sister telling everybody to pray, and seeing some kids holding on to the statue of the Virgin Mary while they were praying. I stood up and turned around. The boy behind me was prepared to walk out of the room. In those days during a fire drill, you were supposed to put your hands on your chest so you wouldn't touch anybody as you went out. He had his hands on his chest. I sat in the middle of the room toward the back. At that point, kids started to move toward the windows. I can remember praying for a little bit, and I thought, well, the firemen will come, they'll put out the fire, and we'll walk out the doors.

But soon I realized that wasn't going to happen. It started to get darker in the room. My sister and I found each other, and I remember being by the window with her. By that time it was chaos. Kids jumping on each other at the windows. These are details that are still with me . . . it was getting so hot in there that the wood around the windowsills was starting to burn and the flames hadn't even reached them. There was a row of kids in front of me and my sister, but we happened to get up to the window. I turned around and started to see flames. That's when the reality of the thing set in. I told my sister, "We have to get outta here. We have to jump." She said she wasn't going to jump. She was scared and crying. I think I got pushed ahead of her at the window. I lost contact with her then. The first half of my body was hanging out the window, but to this day I don't remember telling myself, "I'm going to jump." I might have been pushed out. I think I went out head first, did a somersault in the air going by the first-floor window, and landed on my feet and fell over on my back.

I didn't break any bones when I hit that hard ground. I got up, walked over to the wall of the candy store, and sat there for a couple of minutes. It looked like a war zone. Then I just started walking home. We lived at 3804 West Chicago Avenue, in an apartment over a shoe store. I remember walking past the school on the west side of Avers, which was chaotic with firemen. I saw them pulling out that iron gate in front of the courtyard. But I kept going. I think I just wanted to remove myself from the whole thing. At that point I didn't know what had happened to my sister or my brother Billy, who was in an eighth-grade room. I was just hoping they got out, but neither of them did.

From Avers I headed south down the alley adjacent to the convent. The alley led to the backyard of our place on Chicago Avenue. I think a neighbor saw me when I was about halfway home and brought me to our apartment. My mother was there, and my father was over at the school looking for us. He was a truck driver but was unemployed at the time. My mother asked me if I had seen Billy or Joanne. I told her about Joanne, that I had told her to jump and that I didn't see her after that. I didn't see Billy either. He was across the hallway from us. I remember all the turmoil in our house, trying to find out where they were at. My dad then was checking the hospitals to see if he could find them. My mother stayed home as neighbors and some relatives came over to visit. I had a little burn on my ankle, maybe about three inches in diameter, so they took me over to Garfield Park Hospital. The doctor said it looked like I had been burned by the radiator near the windows.

I pretty much accepted the fact when I was in that room that I was going to die. I was just hoping it would be fast. I wasn't a brave kid. I ended up at that window, and I was pushed out.

The deaths of Joanne and Billy affected my father terribly. He used to be the biggest jokester and was always goofing around. But after the fire, he changed dramatically. He was very angry. I think he was angry at the Catholic church, at God. My mother stayed pretty much the same, and she accepted it more than my father. She was not a real religious lady, but she used to go to church regularly. I didn't go to any of the wakes for the other kids. My brother and sister were waked at Rago Funeral Home on Western Avenue, and that was the extent of my going to wakes. Joanne and Billy were buried at Mt. Carmel Cemetery.

In talking about my father being angry, I remember one time when I used to play on Avers—this would be the summer after the fire—that there was some kind of commotion at the rectory where the police came for some reason. I actually thought it was my father going over there to get at one of the priests. His anger hadn't left him. In my mind, I thought, geez, my father's over there trying to kill somebody. It was hard watching my mother and father go through the grieving, but I was too young to form any ideas about the effect the fire had on people. The resentment and anger didn't really hit me until later in life. When I had children of my own, I could imagine much better what my parents went through in losing my brother and sister.

After the fire I went to Our Lady Help of Christians and then to Orr public school. Three or four of my friends from our room at OLA were gone . . . Peter Cangelosi, who lived on our block; Victor Jacobellis, Joseph Modica. I didn't go back to the new school. We moved out of the neighborhood in 1960, to around Diversey and Austin. I finished grammar school at St. Ferdinand's in 1963 and went to St. Patrick High School, graduating from there in 1967.

I don't know whether I should get into this part of my life, but I became involved with alcohol and drug abuse at a young age. I'm not ashamed of it today because I've been sober for many years. But there were many years of drinking. In looking back, when I was old enough to develop my own thoughts and ideas, I had a lot of resentment. I had a lot of fear. I was loaded with self-pity and guilt. Did the fire make me drink and use drugs? I don't know. In those days in the sixties and seventies, a lot of people were doing those things. But it sure didn't help me. I belong to Alcoholics Anonymous and have been sober since 1987. I still go to AA meetings. It's funny, but I've run into a lot of people at AA who were in that fire.

Today I have two children of my own, Andrew and Deana. Two years ago I got divorced after twenty-four years of marriage.

Andrew's nineteen and he lives with me in Bloomingdale. Deana is twenty-two and works in New York. I'm glad they never had to go through something like I did.

Today I don't have any anger or resentment toward anybody. The fire happened. I was there. It was unfortunate. It's a fact of life. We were just at the wrong place at the wrong time, but so were a lot of other people. I think of the nun in my room. She had fifty-five kids who were freaking out. How do you deal with that? I believe she did the best job she could under awful circumstances. That fire traveled so fast.

What happened at Our Lady of the Angels should never be forgotten, especially the kids and nuns who died and all the others with long-term injuries. And families who lost loved ones, too. The most horrible thing about it for me, though, was watching my mother and father grieve when I was growing up. That's what sticks in my mind after all these years.

Patricia Rice, R.N.

✤

She was on duty as a senior nursing student at St. Anne's Hospital on the day of the fire. The hospital, which closed in 1988, was located at 4950 West Thomas Street, some sixteen blocks from Our Lady of the Angels School. Today she works at Evanston Northwestern Healthcare in quality management, dealing with patient safety at three different north suburban hospitals. A former associate professor at the School of Nursing at St. Xavier College (now university) in Chicago, she lives in Knollwood, Illinois, "with my female partner and two cats."

Memories of that day and night have stayed with me through all these years. I was nineteen years old at the time. I was born in the Austin neighborhood, near St. Anne's Hospital. After graduating from Lourdes High School, I went to St. Anne's to become a nursing student. It was an inexpensive way to get an education. It was all that I could afford.

The afternoon of the fire I remember that we first heard the doorbell ringing, then pounding, and then a man shouting, "Open up! Open up! I've got lots of kids here, and they're all burned!"

We pushed open the emergency room doors and kicked down the doorstops that would hold them in that position for many hours to come. I don't remember if the first vehicle to arrive was a passenger car or one of the Cadillac-style ambulances the Fire Department used in 1958. My memories of the children inside are clear, however. They weren't lying on stretchers. They rode sitting up, some of them on one another's laps.

"It was packed," my classmate Carol recalled. "I thought they'd never stop getting out of there."

The most seriously injured in this first group sat in front with the driver. He returned to his vehicle and lifted out a nine-year-old girl who would be among the most seriously burned of all the children who came through the ER that afternoon. He carried her into the first examining room, and Carol and I followed. We got her name and tried to explain what we were going to do. She had been burned about the face and scalp, and her features were white, waxy, and swollen under a layer of soot. The idea of having her clothes cut off terrified her. She alternately pleaded not to be hurt further and begged us to help her. "I'll give you all my money if you'll just help me," she said.

Carol was concerned about her eyes and put in a call for an ophthalmologist while I tried to calm the girl. It seemed a very long time before other team members arrived to evaluate the child and transport her to surgery. But according to a published account, the triage team was assembled and functioning within fifteen minutes.

Meanwhile the other children had been helped into wheelchairs and onto carts and examining tables. One or two severely injured children can easily monopolize the resources of an average community hospital emergency room. St. Anne's would admit thirty-four children and three nuns by early evening, and nine of them would still be on the critical list three days later. Nine more children would be treated and released. About ten other children were dead on arrival or died before being admitted.

Because the children arrived during a change of shift, many of the more experienced staff nurses—who worked from 7 to 3 p.m.—were sent to the ER where physician-nurse teams worked with each child. Nursing students were then assigned to transport supplies and children. My feeling now is that I didn't know what the hell I was doing. I was trying to find linens, I was trying to find dressings, cotton balls, syringes. Frankly, I was in a state of panic.

Some incoming casualties were sent directly to the operating room while others were dispatched to the Amberg auditorium in the school of nursing to await treatment for non-life-threatening injuries. While I was chasing down supplies, Carol accompanied a child to the auditorium. In contrast to the apparent confusion in the emergency room, she recalls things were pretty well organized in the auditorium, where each child was attended by a member of the staff or a nursing student.

"Those who could," Carol said, "were anxious to tell their stories, to tell us what happened." Kids with fractures talked about how they had jumped. One kid talked about the man who caught him. He was very excited about that. He had fractures, but he kept saying, "I didn't get burned. I wasn't burned." The man himself was admitted to the hospital that night for back injuries sustained during his rescue efforts.

An important feature of a hospital disaster plan is a communications system to recall physicians and needed staff, and to make information about casualties available. Because the hospital switchboard was tied up with incoming calls from parents and the press, telephone lines were not available for hospital use. A nursing school faculty member had to use a phone in the little room behind the switchboard to call other hospitals. "I had to try to get lists of patients who had been admitted elsewhere," she said, "because we had so many families hunting for their children." I'll never forget her use of the word "hunting."

At St. Anne's, parents were sent to the "blue room," a lounge in the nursing school. "We didn't know the names of many of the children, they were so seriously burned," recalled Sister Stephen, director of the nursing school. "I was trying to read a list of the ones whose names we had. I couldn't pronounce some of them, so I asked one of the parents to help. I'll never forget how he read his own child's name, and then he broke down."

A nursing student came in with the names of those admitted elsewhere. "I had to stand on a chair to read the list," she said. "Parents whose children weren't on any of the lists had to be advised to go to the County Morgue."

"Crowds in the main lobby. People crying. People crying. The smell was overwhelming," said a junior nursing student. "I was assigned to a seventh-grade girl who had jumped. She had a fractured pelvis and second-degree burns over about 10 percent of her body. Her parents were hysterical all night long, but she was calm. Too calm, actually. I think she would have been better off if she'd been more upset or angry. We were told very little about what to do. I was given her charts with the doctor's orders and told to stay. Each child had his or her own nurse, many of them student nurses. The severely burned kids had more experienced staff, and student nurses were assigned to assist."

One junior nursing student, assigned to a severely burned child, recalled "the physical suffering of the children and the emotional suffering of families. There were parents and priests all over the place, going in and out of rooms, looking for children. It was shocking to hear a parent saying, 'I think this is my child, but I'm not sure.'"

By ten o'clock that night, every patient admitted had been transported to a room in a patient-care area. The crowds had cleared from the main corridor, and order was slowly being restored in the emergency room. But things would not return to normal at St. Anne's for a long time.

The medical staff formed teams that made rounds on each child every three hours. Each team signed out to the oncoming team. Doctors were coming in and out, day and night, showing their devotion and their care. Contact with the children's own family physicians was maintained as a professional courtesy and as a source of comfort and continuity of care for families.

Initially many children were treated with ointments and dressings—the so-called closed method of treating burns. After consultation with army surgeons and navy burn specialists, the decision was made to switch to an "open method," placing seriously burned children between layers of sterile bed linens on Stryker frames. The change in treatment meant, for many, that ointments and dressings had to be removed. Children were placed in protective isolation to reduce the probability of fatal infections, and pharmaceutical houses supplied us with new, stronger antibiotics. The Chicago community expressed its grief with an outpouring of gifts for the children and financial assistance for the families. Appeals were made for blood donors, and four collection centers were established citywide. Prisoners at Cook County Jail volunteered to donate blood, along with men and women from every corner of the city. Some called to offer their skin for grafts. One group donated money to purchase the latest in surgical skin-grafting equipment.

During the days that followed the fire, at the hospital we settled into a routine. The psychological impact of the burn patients began to be felt by nursing students and members of the staff. "At first," a student nurse said, "I felt helpless. I was only twenty years old. I had experienced the death of someone I knew. I had had polio myself, and knew others who died of it. But I was feeling overwhelmed by the fear that, in caring for the children, we would hurt them more than they were already hurt."

Another student nurse grieved for the memory of a child she had cared for who died much later. "It has a terrible psychological effect," she said, "caring for a child who suffered that long and still died."

Almost every one of the nurses reported strong emotional reactions, many of them delayed for several days, until we finally made contact with the world outside the hospital.

I started to cry about ten o'clock Monday night, after the emergency room was cleared. And I was reprimanded. By the end of the week, when I called home and heard my mother's voice, I burst into tears.

Another nursing student held up until she got home and saw the newspaper reports. "My dad took me to a neighborhood place and bought me a drink," she said. "There I was, sitting at a bar, crying and talking to my dad. He just listened."

One other nursing student had the following week off. "Coming home, seeing the newspapers and watching TV," she said, "I experienced a delayed reaction. I got real upset. When we all came back on Sunday night, we found we'd all had the same experience. In retrospect it taught me something. People said, 'How can you deal with all that sorrow?' I think that when you are in control, when you are able to do something, you can cope."

I was fond of saying that the things we saw at the hospital on the day of the school fire did not affect me. I didn't have nightmares. I didn't have bad dreams. But afterwards I sure as hell didn't go into emergency nursing, and I didn't go near a burn unit. I just avoided getting involved in emergency or trauma care. I kept myself away from that for the rest of my life.

If we get another major disaster in Chicago with mass casualties, we'll be no better equipped to handle it than we were at St. Anne's—unless we support our trauma system. That support is absolutely essential in a metropolitan area that has two airports and so many large public gathering places.

In 1958 there was no burn center in the city of Chicago. I still think sadly about the children from Our Lady of the Angels who were burned, especially Michele McBride, who was cared for at our hospital for several months. Many years later we went out and had dinner together a couple of times, and it was obvious that she was still troubled by what had happened to her.

I think the church's response to the school fire left a great deal to be desired. It's one thing for the cardinal to walk through the hospital and bless the kids, but there was no notion of talking about it. The church treated the burned kids like it treated the kids who complained of sex abuse. Church officials didn't want to talk about it. They made people feel like they weren't entitled to be sad and to be angry, and to ask questions. That was a time when you didn't ask questions of your church.

I think St. Anne's acquitted itself well in handling the heavy load of injured kids from the school fire. That's not just school pride on my part. If we had had a field triage system at that time, the situation would have been much less chaotic. A team on the site, looking at the casualties and being in touch with the hospital, would know if the hospital was overloaded. If it was, the victims could be sent elsewhere. At our hospital, the kids just kept coming and coming—in cars, in ambulances—and we had to take them without any clear notion of what other hospitals were ready to do.

Michael Cannella

"After the fire, I grew up with my mother crying herself to sleep every night," he says, "and I'm very angry about what it did to our family." He lives in Rochelle, a town west of De Kalb, Illinois, and has an adult son and daughter. After working as a mover for thirty-seven years, he is now a full-time musician and has a partnership in a recording studio. "Even though he's gone, I've never stopped talking to my brother George," he adds. "But I've never told people that because they'd think I'm crazy. I'm the only one in our family who didn't cry. I'd say, 'George ain't dead. He's okay. He's with the angels. We're the ones in trouble.'"

At the time of the fire I was only a little kid in first grade, away from the main school building, but my older brother, George III, was in fifth grade [Room 212]. It happened eleven days before I was six years old. Basically, before the fire we had a happy home. After my brother died, it was a house of crying. It hit all of us hard, but my mother could never stop crying. My mother's name was Angela, and my father, George II, is still living. He is eighty-eight and lives in a retirement home in Northlake. My mother died in

2000. She was eighty-four. She's buried right next to Georgie now.

On the day of the fire we wound up in neighboring houses where people came looking for their kids. Parents were fainting everywhere because they couldn't find their children. I think my aunt or my sister Marlene came and got me from school. Whoever it was took me to my aunt's house, because my mother was at the hospital where they had taken my brother and were trying to revive him. What I later heard was that he died in my mother's arms. I was told she kept telling the doctors to keep trying, keep trying to keep George alive. But he didn't make it. He didn't have a mark on him when he died. He died from smoke inhalation. He was ten years old.

Our family lived at 1145 North Harding, but we moved out of the neighborhood in 1959. My ma couldn't stop her grieving. So my dad moved us out to Villa Park. We were in one of the first houses out there. That's where I grew up, Villa Park and Lombard, those two suburbs. My mother stopped crying during the day, but at night she still cried herself to sleep. You could hear her words, "Georgie, Georgie," every night. Then it got to be not every night but still most of the time. My father was usually just comforting my mother and holding things together so they wouldn't get worse. It was so traumatic for my mother, I don't think any of us even wanted to cry and make it worse for her. My mother was the old-school Sicilian—a stay-at-home mother, bake cookies every day. She believed that when you met someone you should always leave them feeling happier and better.

I can remember stealing ice off the ice truck with Georgie. He'd put me on the handlebars of his bike with his buddies following us. When the ice man climbed up the stairs of an apartment building with big chunks of ice, my brother pedaled us next to the truck, gave me a chisel, and had me cut off pieces from the ice stacked on the truck and hand them off to the other kids. My alibi was "my big brother made me do it."

My sister Marlene and I didn't discuss the school fire. She was in one of the classrooms where everybody got out. She says, "I helped raise you, and you helped raise Ronnie," my younger brother. Ronnie was born in 1956. As he grew up, I had to help keep him in line because my parents didn't have it in them to discipline him—probably because they had lost George, and the fact that my father had to work two jobs to make ends meet, so he was away from home a lot.

Every Sunday we went to the Mt. Carmel Cemetery. We'd have a picnic there, stay until the place closed. My dad had a hundred-foot hose and a sprinkler, and we had the greenest grass by my brother's gravesite. And the flowers. My mother would always bring fresh flowers. The ritual never bored me. My brother and I, we'd take off for hours and climb every tree in that cemetery. That little stone entrance—we used to climb up on top of it. You can see Georgie's monument right away. It's one street north of Roosevelt Road. It's about eight feet by five feet high. It's got a big image of the Infant Jesus carved in there. About a hundred feet west is the gravesite of Al Capone.

As we got older, into our teens, my brother and I talked our mother out of going to the cemetery all the time. When our parents were away from the house, we'd put on the boxing gloves and go at it. In those days boxing was an "in" sport because it was on TV. Our dad had bought us boxing gloves, so we often punched each other around. It was a way for me to straighten Ronnie out if he was doing something wrong. Eventually he got bigger, maybe a foot taller than me. One day he says, "Now, I'm gonna get ya." He's beatin' the hell out of me. He's hurtin' me bad. So I hit him in the head and knocked him out. We're on the second floor of the house, and all of a sudden my dad comes in from the cemetery. He says, "Tell your brother to come on downstairs, we've got something for him." They'd bought him something from a discount store. "Aw, Dad," I said, "he's sleepin'."

"Well, get him up," he says. I went and got a pitcher of water. I said, "I think he's thirsty." I went upstairs and threw the water on his face, saying to myself, "God, don't have him dead on me, I'll never hit my brother again as long as I live." I dumped the water on him, and he woke up and didn't know what happened. I've never touched my brother since then. What would I tell my parents, that I killed their youngest son? That's the kind of effect the school fire had on my life.

I've written many songs about the kids who died in the fire. I haven't published them yet because I was working hard as a teamster, didn't have the money to do it, and was helping raise a son and daughter. Those angels are gone, but they're not dead. They are still with us.

I think anyone who had any connection to the school fire should share their memories. You can't lock them up. My memories of losing my brother and of watching my mother suffer so much, of watching her throw herself onto Georgie's grave after the funeral, have brought me close to God.

Ken Leonard

❧

*A last-minute survivor of a room that suffered thirty
fatalities and fifteen injured students, he resides in a
comfortable home in Oak Lawn, a suburb southwest of
Chicago. He spent only a short time as a student at OLA,
but memories of his escape and rescue remain etched in his
mind. He retired as assistant chief of the Oak Lawn Fire
Department in 2001.*

I was nine years old in the fourth grade, Room 210, on the
north side of the school. Sister Mary Seraphica was assign-
ing us some homework just before school got out when almost simultaneously everyone noticed smoke coming into
the room. There were doors at the front and back of the
room, and both had transoms. We noticed this thick black
smoke coming in from under the front door. I remember
one of the students closest to the door yelling, "Fire!" There
was some commotion, and the nun advised everyone to get
back in their seats. She got up from her desk, went to the
rear of the room, and opened the door. By this time the
smoke had moved down the hall, and when she opened
the door the smoke came pouring into the room.

Sister closed the door and turned around, and she was just as black as her habit. Her face and hands were sooty. That's when pandemonium started to break out. She got everyone back into their seats, returned to the front of the room, and instructed us to start to pray. I believe she wanted us to say the Hail Mary. This lasted probably less than thirty seconds when the smoke started coming in through the transoms and it began getting difficult to breathe. Students started going toward the windows and opening them. I sat almost dead-smack in the middle of the room. Danger from the fire and smoke just didn't register with me. I don't know whether I was in shock; I can't really say. But I remained at my desk until I just couldn't breathe anymore. By this time a good part of the class was at the windows. Some students had jumped as I got to the windows myself, fighting to get my head out and breathe some fresh air.

The Fire Department was just arriving. People on the ground were yelling, "Don't jump! Don't jump!" I got myself out onto the windowsill with the intention of jumping. I had pushed kids out of the way to get there. It was a struggle. I was fighting for air. I was very small for my age, and it would have been quite a leap from that windowsill. The alternative wasn't any better. The firemen had a rescue net down there two windows to my left, and I intended to make that jump, but before I could, the net had filled up with other students. I basically froze on the windowsill. In the meantime, students who were behind me in the classroom fighting to get out the window were no longer there. Nobody was left behind me. I don't know whether the room flashed or if the roof came down, but I wasn't looking back.

Flames started coming through the window, and that's when my legs were burned while I stood on the windowsill. A fireman's hose knocked the flames down behind me, and simultaneously another fireman had thrown up a ladder, came up, bodily grabbed me off the windowsill, and brought me down.

In the crowd on the ground I ran into my two brothers who were also in the school at the time, but they had gotten out of the building quite quickly. Michael was in fifth grade, and my brother Bob was in sixth. They were uninjured. They saw me frozen on the windowsill and told me they were frantically trying to get my attention. "We kept yelling at you," they said, but I didn't see them. I was mesmerized.

We got together and just decided to walk home at that point. We lived at 3636 West Chicago Avenue. I was soaking wet, and the back of my pants were burned off. We got about a block away from the school when a police officer in a squad car noticed us, me in particular, picked us up, and took us home. My mother was at work at the time. When our next-door neighbor saw me, she immediately took me in and put me in a tub of warm water.

From that point I don't know whether it was by ambulance or exactly who took me to the hospital. But I ended up eventually at Franklin Boulevard Hospital. I had burns from the knees down to the ankles on both legs. My mother, Dorothy, was a single parent at the time—my parents divorced when I was three or four years old. Coming home from work at Western Electric at 22nd and Cicero, my mother was on the bus when she saw the smoke in the distance. Somebody on the bus said, "That's Our Lady of the Angels. It's on fire." She immediately jumped off the bus and ran three or four blocks to the school, looked for me for a while, and then ran all the way to our apartment. The little girl next door who was my age met her at the top of the stairs and told her I was in the hospital. At that point my mother passed out. Upon awakening, she began her search again and at midnight finally found me. I spent that evening in the hospital. They released me the next day because there certainly were kids more injured than me who needed immediate care. I had second-degree burns. The doctors wanted to see how I was doing, so my mother took me back to the hospital and they kept me for another ten days.

I believe it was shortly after Christmas that we resumed school. Some of the neighboring Chicago public schools had classrooms that we used. I went to Cameron. I finished out the school year, but those months are pretty much a blur to me. That summer in 1959, my mother remarried and we moved to Oak Lawn. I've been here ever since.

After army service in Vietnam, I decided to go to Moraine Valley College on the GI Bill. I went there almost two years but was just short of getting a degree. I was doing odd jobs at the time, getting money from the GI Bill to pay the rent and stuff like that. Through some acquaintances I found out that the Oak Lawn Fire Department was taking applications, so I applied for the opening in 1975 and was hired. I was with the department for twenty-six years and retired in 2001 as an assistant chief.

I have three stepchildren and six grandchildren, and they all live right here in Oak Lawn. I've never talked much in detail to them about the fire, just the highlights of what happened. It's like talking about Vietnam to some kids today: you don't go into it.

The fire was quite hard on my mother. We had virtually no conversation about it unless I brought it up. Being a single mother with four children, she went through a lot of stress and anxiety at the time. She asked me only once what I did that day, but we never had any conversation in depth about it.

During my time with the Fire Department we never had any bad fires, certainly nothing like some they had in Chicago and absolutely nothing like what happened at Our Lady of the Angels. In my final position with the department, I was in charge of our training academy. We would get fire candidates from all over northern Illinois for the six-week sessions. I would relate to them the story of the school fire. In fact, every class went out and bought *To Sleep with the Angels* and asked me to autograph the book.

After all these years I still have feelings of sadness about the school fire. There's not one December 1 that I don't recall the fire. My thoughts and memories are the same as they were many years ago. What happened to me is still very vivid. Fortunately I was so centered on survival that either I put out of my mind or ignored any memory of what the other children went through. But I do recall seeing girls with their hair on fire jumping out the windows. It doesn't bother me when I think about it even though it was a horrific experience, but I may have blocked out a lot of things I saw. Even to this day I find myself getting emotional talking about it. At every graduating class at the academy I would relate the story, and I would have a hard time getting through it without having to excuse myself.

When I think back about my days at Our Lady of the Angels, I know it was our first year in that parish. And the fire was three months into the school year. I had become

kind of a teacher's pet, if you will. I was in charge of empty-
ing the wastebaskets and beating the erasers outside. Each
day I would go down those staircases where the fire came
up, go out with the trash, smack the erasers together, and
come back up with them. That particular day, that would
have been the time I would have done those chores, just
before school was over. To this day I don't know why Sister
didn't have me do it. I do recall one time there was a pile
of cardboard underneath the stairs. Being nine years old, it
didn't make any sense to me. I never figured out it might
be a fire hazard.

Since I was in the school for only three months and we
left the neighborhood the next year, I didn't maintain a
close association with students in my class. If I could look
at a class picture, I maybe could pick out two or three kids
I tried to be friends with; but when I read the names of
those that perished in my room, I can't put a face to most
of them.

In retrospect my life has been good, except for some
cancer problems I've been fighting, but I'm very proud of
the fact I ended up with the Fire Department. It wasn't
something I ever dreamed of doing, having been in the
school fire. There wasn't any connection. It was just fate or
whatever you want to call it, but I was able to help some
people on my end of the deal while in the fire service.

I've been asked if something like the school fire could
happen again, and I say, certainly things have changed, but
we can't get lackadaisical about safety precautions because
we seem doomed to repeat history. With terrorism such a
big deal now, we can't let our guard down, especially when
it comes to protecting our kids.

Father Pat McPolin

*A priest belonging to the Claretian religious order, he served
as a chaplain with the Chicago Police Department from
1943 to 1952 and again from 1956 to 1965. Born in St.
Brendan Parish on the South Side of the city in 1916, he
lived last spring in the Little Sisters of the Poor nursing
home in San Pedro, California. In 1965 he left Chicago after
being appointed head of the Claretian Western Province, and
was based in Los Angeles. Among his many close friends in
the entertainment community was actor Danny Thomas.*

There was a luncheon that day in one of the big hotels
downtown. Tom Lyons, chief of the uniformed force of the
Chicago Police Department, was there. As the police chaplain, I was asked to give the invocation. After I did that, I
stayed for lunch and sat at a side table. During the proceed-
ings, someone got to Chief Lyons and told him, "There's
a big fire going on at a school on the West Side," and the
police had ordered a disaster plan put into effect.

So the chief left the speakers' table, and as he came
down he said to me, "We're going to need your help too."
I joined him as he went downstairs and briefed me about

the fire. His chauffeur dropped me off at 221 West Madison Street where I had parked my chaplain's car, at the St. Jude Police League.

I hopped in the car—a souped-up Oldsmobile—turned on the red flasher, and used all my emergency privileges in speeding to the fire. I was never known for being a slow driver—I think I must've been going sixty miles an hour. I believe I went west on Warren Boulevard, through Garfield Park out to Hamlin Avenue because there was no truck traffic going that way. I got out to the school maybe about 3:20 p.m. Police ambulances and fire trucks galore were all over the area.

An officer told me that the fire was virtually out by this time, and that there were kids inside the building. The ones who jumped out or were rescued had been taken to hospitals. I saw the parish priests anointing each body as it was being carried out of the school. The number of ambulances and emergency vehicles was tremendous, and the thing I remember at the time was that nobody was telling them which way to go—just get to a hospital, even though some of the kids looked like they were dead.

In view of the fact the priests were there and taking charge of doing the anointing, I was more or less an observer to what was going on. It was chilly, and it got dark early. They had big floodlights to illuminate the place. Fire people were going through the school, room by room. There were parents all over, looking for their kids. Police couldn't help them because they didn't know which ambulance went where. They didn't take the names of any of the kids, figuring the hospitals would do that.

A disaster plan was in effect, but it wasn't coordinated at first. Soon the order went out to take all dead bodies to the County Morgue. I was informed then that it was going to be a police problem, because identification of bodies is a police responsibility. "Father," they told me, "you're going to be needed over there. It's going to be a mob scene, with parents looking for their children."

I already knew some kids had been taken to the morgue because there was communication by radio between the hospitals and squadrols. So I got back in my car and drove to the morgue. I got there by around 6 p.m. or a little later. I don't know what the record shows about the first arrivals, but some bodies were there when I arrived. The morgue workers had cots, like skids, that were placed row upon row, covered with white sheets. As the ambulances and squadrols pulled up with more bodies, I couldn't believe what I saw. It seemed like they never stopped. Tears were streaming down the face of a policeman who was carrying in a body. "I'm thinking of my kids," he said.

It was going on seven o'clock when parents started to arrive. Before they were let into that big room in the morgue, a few nuns from the school came in and were able to identify some of the children. "Oh, no!" a nun said, evidently recognizing one of her former students. She broke down right there. It was a child she knew, or knew her family. By 7:30 the majority of the bodies had been laid out. I was asked to take part in the identification process. I had a piece of paper someplace in my belongings and used it to scribble down some notes. About four or five o'clock the next morning, my hands were greasy and black from touching human, burned flesh, and those notes still had grease on them.

They asked us to start the identification systematically because they couldn't take every parent in at once. They told us to make notes that would help in identifying the child. You could hardly tell in some cases whether it was a nine-year-old or an eleven-year-old, a boy or a girl. We jotted down things like color of hair, items of clothing, jewelry, type of medal, color of socks. In most cases, shoes had come off, but there were socks still on some of them. Clothing was burned off some of the victims.

Later we went over to the waiting room where parents were gathering. Some of them had been to hospitals, hadn't found their children, and had come to the morgue expecting the worst. They were just beyond themselves with sorrow, not knowing whether their children were there or in a hospital they had missed.

We would give a description of some identifying item from the kids and say, "A boy with brown loafers and brown corduroy pants, wearing a St. Christopher medal." In the beginning they'd take a father and mother in together to see the victims, but it got too pathetic because the mothers would break down when they went into the room and saw all these bodies. Most of the time it was just taking the fathers through. The coroner's office had all kinds of assistants to help.

They brought the bodies of the nuns into a small separate room. One of the nuns was almost completely burned. She still had on a heavy belt that the nuns wear, and her clothing was identifiable. A nun who was at the morgue to help in the identification came with a laundry list. I remember that part of the underclothing of the nun who died was protected under that black belt and had a laundry number on it. That's how her identity was assured.

It was well after midnight when we got to the bodies of the students who had few if any identifying marks—just one shoe, a sock. How many kids wore blue stockings or socks? Somebody from the coroner's office gave us little wooden tongue depressors that doctors use. We used them to open a victim's mouth to see the teeth, because it wasn't common then for children to have braces. Some of them did, though, or the parent would know from the teeth. They knew, for instance, that Johnny had a crooked tooth in front.

Because of the heat, some of the faces had assumed a kind of mummified look. The jaws seemed to shrink, but the mouth would be protruding and the lips would be kind of tight. Sometimes you would open an eye so the parent could see the color, whether it was blue or brown. This was the hardest part of the ordeal for the parents as well as for us.

I left the morgue after about twelve hours. My work was pretty much done. I left a little after six that morning. I went to St. Francis of Assisi Church on Roosevelt Road, near Halsted. I lived in the rectory there. I had 6:30 Mass.

As I was freshening up before putting on my vestments for the Mass, I was numb, completely numb. The shock hit me hard when I looked at my hands. They were darkened with human oil.

At the morgue, some of the policemen didn't want to go home right away. They didn't want to meet their families because they felt the look of death was on their faces. Some of the guys told me that later. "Father," they said, "I couldn't go home. I was with death. I'd be afraid to look at my own kids. I was afraid that what I saw would be pouring out of my eyes." Their words remained with me for many years.

I told more than one policeman that night, "You keep up your spirit, you don't go to pieces now because you are doing a work of mercy. It's your job. We've got to help these people."

At the Mass that morning, my prayers were not only for the kids. They were in the Lord's hands. I think I prayed more for their parents who were suffering so greatly from the tragedy.

In all the years I was police chaplain, I walked hand in hand with death and sorrow. Many times I had to break the news of an officer killed in the line of duty to his wife and kids. I was on call twenty-four hours a day, never knowing when a call would take me to some terrible accident or killing of an officer.

But of all the experiences I had in trying to bring comfort and encouragement to others in times of tragedy, none ever affected me as much as the work I did that night at the morgue.

Albin Anderson

✥

A native of the city's Northwest Side, he was twenty-eight years old on the day of the fire and a member of rescue Squad 6, which raced to the school on the box alarm. Today he lives with his wife, Jeanette, in Nelson, Wisconsin, where he operates a large farm. He says he'll never forget seeing "some kids still sitting at their desks" as he sloshed his way into a water-soaked room to recover bodies of eighth-grade students.

We came in and parked on Iowa Street. We pulled up in front of the church because we had been given the wrong address, 3808 West Iowa. The kids were running out of the church doors, and we went in because that's where we figured the fire was. The kids we saw were all sooty and dirty from smoke. I don't know who it was, but someone kept shouting to us, "No, the other way, the other way!" So we ran around the corner and got into the courtyard where we raised two ladders to windows of the second-floor room on the west end of the north wing of the building. I got up on one ladder and grabbed a kid by the belt. I don't know why I couldn't get him out because I had a good grip on him. I was ducking low. The flames were actually coming out the bottom half of the window. The back of the boy's head was burned, his hair was crinkled. He was obviously dead. There was nothing I could do about it. I looked down, and Lieutenant Jack McCone was there at the foot of the ladder. He nodded to me, and I pushed the boy back in so it wouldn't look so terrible to the neighborhood people below, seeing the boy hanging out that window, completely limp and lifeless.

As I recall, we helped kids who had jumped out and were lying injured in the courtyard. Later on we went in to recover bodies, and the water in that one room I worked was quite deep. A few kids were still slumped on their desks, and that's something I'll never forget, but most of them were just lying in the water or stacked like cordwood up against the windowsills. I remember seeing the kid that I tried to pull out—he was there in that pile below the window. I could hardly believe it when I saw the other few kids still at their desks. Those two doors on the second floor were so close to the front stairs [that led to Avers Avenue], they could've been used as an escape route for kids in a couple of the rooms [211 and 212]. If the nuns had just let the kids out right away, told them to get out, those rooms would've been emptied.

In our recovery work we scooped up the bodies of the kids and carried them out to other men in the hallway. Afterward we went into the basement of the school and pumped water out of the boiler room. We did general cleanup stuff and didn't get back to our station until about eleven o'clock that night. Our station was at Stave Street and Prindiville, where we quartered with members of Engine 43. We didn't have much conversation about the fire. We all had our own thoughts about what we had seen. My youngest daughter,

Susan, was only about six months old. Some of the men in the department had children the same age as the kids who died or were injured, so they probably had a stronger emotional reaction. But it hit me pretty hard too. As I recall, a couple of days later we went to Engine 85's station to make our formal reports. I know McCone, Bill Mueller, and myself were there. It took a couple of hours. Somebody took a picture of the three of us, looking at what was supposed to be a blueprint of the school building. But it was only a big sheet of paper to make it look official.

It's hard at this time to remember a lot of things I did at the fire. I'm seventy-eight now. It sort of reminds me of what Mark Twain once said about remembering stuff. He said the older he gets, the better his memory is because he's even remembering things that never happened. But I do know I was there with a lot of other people, doing our best to save or help the kids.

I retired from the Fire Department in 1988. To be honest, I don't think about the school fire much anymore. As harsh an experience as it was, you can't let it control your thoughts and everyday life. Many of the firemen who were there that day are gone now. As I say, it's nice to be alive— so many of us aren't.

When I joined the Fire Department in January 1956, I weighed 151 pounds, and when I left the department I weighed 151 pounds. Since then I've blown up, and I'm about 158 now!

When I was in my mid-twenties, one of my friends, Bill Frawley, wanted to sign up for the department, and he asked me to go down with him. He wanted me to drive his car around the block while he went in to fill out the application. I don't think he had enough money to park the car in a garage. When we got downtown, he found a parking space, so I went in with him. It cost, I think, three bucks at the time to fill out an application, so I filled one out too. I eventually got on the Fire Department, and my friend didn't. How's that for an odd twist?

I grew up around Central and Diversey in Chicago, went to Steinmetz High School where I graduated in 1948. I then became a seaman, working on the Great Lakes for a couple of summers. We carried ore and grain; I worked as a coal passer. In 1950 I became a fireman on an engine with the Chicago, Milwaukee, St. Paul and Pacific railroad. The only reason I went on the job was that my father wanted me to do it; he was a railroad engineer. He thought railroad was the way to go. I joined the Marine Corps in 1951, and in 1952 went over to Korea where we came in at Inchon. I saw some action as a forward observer for the artillery, and finished my tour of duty as a corporal.

Thinking back on that day of the school fire, I still believe a lot of kids in those two rooms on the second floor could have escaped if the nuns hadn't kept them in their seats. It showed how strict the discipline was in Catholic schools in those days. You have to feel sorry about what happened, but at the time there was a lot of anger among firemen after what we saw. Everybody felt bad, but you were just mad because so many kids died when they didn't have to. A key part of the whole story, of course, is the fact the fire had such a head start before the alarm came in. The Friends of OLA have sent me their newsletter, telling me about their meetings and reunions. And every year I send them a donation to show my appreciation of their good work. They deserve credit for keeping alive memories of the children and nuns who died in the fire.

Maureen Bailey Bidwell

✿

A registered nurse, she lives with her husband Harry in Mount Vernon, Illinois. Although she escaped safely from the school fire, she says the event affected her life in many ways. Now a grandmother, she works in a hospital five days a week from 7 a.m. to 3:30 p.m. or later depending on the circumstances, and reminds nurses she trains of the constant need for caution regarding fire regulations.

It happened two weeks before my eleventh birthday. I was in sixth grade. I don't remember the room number [it was 205]. Miss Coughlan was our teacher. I was always very short, so usually I was sitting in a front row, which I was that day, maybe about four rows over from the door. I remember a knock on the door—it was Miss Tristano, the teacher in the room next to ours. When the door was opened, some white smoke drifted into the room. We could see the smoke in the hallway.

[*After the two teachers conferred, Coughlan went to the principal's office on the second floor; but she could not find her because the principal was substituting in another room on the first floor. The rule was that only the principal could ring the school fire alarm.*]

By the time Miss Coughlan started getting us out of the room, the smoke was getting dark. You could hear kids yelling and screaming in the hallway. They were tripping and banging into each other. I was so glad a boy in front of me had on a white shirt, because we couldn't see anything. We were only a few feet from the stairway. The smoke had turned dark so quickly. Everyone was trying to get down the stairs at the same time. It was a little crazy. It was just like a big wave of kids rolling out the door leading to Iowa Street.

Then, in the usual fire-drill fashion, we lined up in front of the church, next to the rectory. I remember standing there, the girl next to me crying because she had left her coat in the building. It was a new coat, her mother had just bought it. I just wanted to hit her. Here kids were trapped in the school, and she was worried about her coat! I think we were already out when the school fire alarm sounded.

We stood there for a little bit. There was such a large group of kids outside that obviously we were getting in the way, and we were told to go home. The Fire Department was just starting to work. With all the kids and spectators, it was growing too crowded. I found a friend of mine, Nancy Courtney, who lived in the general direction of my house. We cut down the alley and literally ran toward Chicago Avenue. My family lived at 842 North Harding. We must have looked very strange, because it was December, it was cold, and we had no coats on. The grandfather of one of the students was walking toward us in the alley. He was Italian, had a very heavy accent, and he wanted to know what we were doing out of school. We started yelling, "The school's on fire!" He must've been at least sixty-five years old, but he began the fastest shuffle toward the school that I ever saw.

We ran down Harding Avenue to my house, and Nancy came in with me. My mother, who was in late pregnancy with my sister Janet, greeted us at the door. She told Nancy to call her mother right away to let her know what was happening and that she was all right. My mom gave her a sweater to wear because she didn't want to wait at our house before going home.

We couldn't find my sister Doreen, who was in a first-grade room right by the front door on the first floor, so I knew she was out. One of the mothers in the neighborhood had a car and was taking a lot of the children home, and that's how Doreen got home. My father was on his way home from work. He just happened to hear about the school fire on the radio in a car next to him. He headed for the nearest parking lot because traffic was all tied up, and he ran home, probably a good mile. He worked at Eastman Kodak, outside of downtown. When he came in, he saw us, my sister and myself, and knew we were okay, but he was as white as a ghost from worry. That's how my dad was. He didn't show a lot of emotion. Then he turned around and headed over to the school. He had gone to that school himself and had graduated from there.

I knew students who were hurt in the fire. I remember Diane Palmisano got her feet burned. Michele McBride, who lived in the neighborhood, suffered burns on her face, legs, and hands. Unfortunately I can't remember a lot of the names, but I do remember sitting in front of the television that evening, listening to Fahey Flynn . . . talking about it. . . . Excuse me, I'm ready to cry. . . . Later that night they were showing pictures on TV, and that's how we recognized a lot of the students who died. They lived down the block or were in rooms on our floor at the school. Fortunately no one in my classroom was injured or killed.

The fire affected my life in many ways. This may sound silly, but I'm very, very fire conscious, to a point where my husband just rolls his eyes and throws up his hands when I talk about it. He says, "What's the matter with you? If you're burning trash, and you have a hose out there, just make sure the water is turned on." If the furnace makes a funny noise, I get all nervous about it. Everything has to be safe. Where I work now, I'm a nurse and educator. I work in surgery at Good Samaritan Hospital in Mount Vernon and I'm the operating room educator. I train all the staff when they come in. I keep drilling it into people's heads that you have to be careful: fire exits can't be blocked, fire extinguishers can't be blocked, don't put equipment in front of the pull boxes. When I talk like this, the staff look at me and probably think, "Relax, woman, we're okay." But you never know. You never know what might happen.

Today, if I'm in a building I look for the little exit signs. I always know where the closest door is when I'm someplace away from home. There was only one door to our classroom at Our Lady of the Angels. We recently moved to another house in Mount Vernon, and it has seven doors. There's no way anybody is going to get trapped in our house.

When I got married, my husband was in the Marine Corps. He later was a teamster, a truck driver, but he's retired now. When he got out of the Marines in 1972 after serving in Vietnam, he returned to the Joliet area. That's where I went to nursing school, at St. Joseph's Hospital School of Nursing. From there I went to work at Loyola

University Medical Center just outside of Chicago. At first I was in an intensive-care unit, and then I transferred to surgery. Loyola has a well-respected burn unit. Part of my training, when I first went into surgery, was to go up to the burn unit where they had an operating room for skin grafts and debridements.

I never thought anything about it until the day I walked up there with the person who was training me. As I walked into the day room where the patients gathered and sat around, I burst into tears. I went into a little supply room and sobbed. I just totally lost it. While I scrubbed in surgery, I cried the whole time. I thought maybe it just caught me by surprise, that I didn't expect it would affect me that way. The next time I had to go up there, I was a little more prepared. I just kept my eyes to the ground, didn't look at anyone sitting there, went into the operating area, did what I had to do, and got out of there. After that I talked to my head nurse and said, "Please don't make me go up there again. It's not that I don't want to do it. It's because I can't."

The scrub person is the one who hands the instruments to the surgeon. When I had to do that, I didn't even look at the patient. I just looked at the table of instruments, and when the surgeon wanted something, I handed it to him. I couldn't look at the burned flesh . . . the smell . . . I just couldn't do it. It was like a flashback to the poor kids who were burned in the school fire. Something hit me right between the eyes.

On the day of the school fire it had to be awfully trying for the personnel at St. Anne's Hospital where they brought some seriously burned students. What's really strange is that one of the nurses at Loyola when I was there was a student nurse at St. Anne's. Her name is Nancy Ceccine. Every year on the first of December, she'd ask me, "Maureen, how are you doing?" I'd say "I'm doing okay, how are you doing?" We had a common connection.

That's something the school fire did. It formed a bond among a lot of people who were touched by it. Nancy and I would just look at each other on the anniversary date—it was like Memorial Day, and our feelings were unspoken. We didn't have to say a word, we knew how we felt about it. But I have to keep telling myself how much good came from it—all the changes in school construction and alarm systems, and the greater safety it helped create for students everywhere.

Edward Glanz

🌿

An executive with Abbott Laboratories for many years, he lives with his wife, Susan, in Grayslake, Illinois, and remains grateful to this day to the firefighter who pulled him from a window of Room 211 shortly before the room exploded in flames. He still wonders why he and his fellow students didn't take the risk of bolting out of the room before heavy smoke engulfed the school's second-floor hallway.

After all these years, I believe something good came out of the fire, namely, the improved safety of our schools. It changed the way new schools were built. A lot of the parish and public schools had to put in sprinkler systems and install fire doors. If we had had a fire door on the second floor at Our Lady of the Angels, everybody would've gotten out. People took fires a lot more seriously after that. We used to go through these fire drills. It was like a joke among the students. You know how kids are—the drills gave us a chance to get away from classes. That attitude changed.

I went through all the grades at OLA. Our whole family did, including my brother and three sisters. That was a special parish. It's unusual to keep friends from grade-school days, but that's the way it has been with many of us. Two of my friends, John Molitor and John Lubke, we see each other quite a bit and do some things together. We've gone to a number of the reunions. It must be some ten years ago that Billy O'Brien put together a reunion, and we had about sixty people from our class attend. That was almost forty years after the fire. In a lot of ways I feel closer to these people now than when we were thirteen years old. What we went through has formed a real bond. I remember after the fire, going to wakes at the different funeral homes. You'd see ten, twelve kids laid out. You'd see the parents you might've known. It was kinda difficult. When you're a kid at that age, you don't necessarily think about the permanence of death. As you get older, you have a better understanding and realize how fortunate you really were.

I sat in the back of Room 211, second seat from the rear door. On the afternoon of the fire, three girls—Karen Hobik, Frances Guzaldo, and Janet Delaria—walked in from the hall. They were in our class and had been out of the room temporarily. They told Sister Helaine there was some light smoke in the hall. I was sitting right near the door where they came in, and when they opened it I could see the smoke. Sister went to the front door. She opened it, closed it, and told us to go to the windows. In retrospect I think Sister Helaine made a huge error in doing that. We probably all could've gotten out right then and there if we had gone immediately into the hall and down the front stairs, which were right next to our room. I'm quite sure Sister second-guessed herself about that many times. If we had only had the guts to run out—but at that stage of your life you listened to the nuns, you didn't disagree with them or disobey them.

When we went to the windows, we tried to warn students in the seventh-grade classroom across the courtyard from us about what was happening. We were yelling to them. It seems like it took us a long time to get their attention. We were probably the first ones—our class I mean—to discover that there was actually a fire, because at that point the smoke was very light. Ironically, two of the girls who first saw the smoke, Karen Hobik and Frances Guzaldo, died in the fire. Janet Delaria survived. I was fortunate in going to the one window where they had a ladder that was long enough. We were in that room at least fifteen minutes before the firemen reached us because they were delayed in knocking down the gate in front of the courtyard. When they got a life net below us, it looked to me, from a height of about thirty-five feet, about the size of a dime. We saw kids who jumped out of the other room [209] to the east of us on that canopy over the door of the annex. Eddie Maggerise was one of them, Jimmy Sturtevant was another. They climbed the fence at the end of the courtyard and got out. I was approximately the twelfth kid who got out of our room. One of them at my window was Jimmy Kowalczyk. I think he was the last one to get out of that window where [Fire Department ladder man] Charlie Kamin was working. The only girl who got out that window was Michele Barale. I remember leaning over, trying to get some air. I wasn't breathing too well. The kids were packed together at the window. Kamin reached over, I held onto him, and he pulled me out. I weighed about 130 pounds, but he swung me around and put me on the ladder. He had extraordinary strength. I'm sure his adrenaline had to be pumping to do what he did. I ended up writing a letter to his daughter after he passed away, expressing my thanks that he had saved me.

When I got down from the ladder, I saw some kids on the ground in the courtyard. One of them was Marne Hudson who had jumped from Room 209. I went to a curb on Avers Street and sat down to get some air. Looking back, I saw flames shooting out of the window of our room where I had just been. For me, life or death was a matter of minutes. I also remember seeing Sister Helaine with a couple of other nuns who were holding her and trying to get her to walk. She was in shock, obviously in pain. She had been burned pretty badly. I think they were taking her to the convent.

I didn't hang around long—I didn't have a coat. I met a friend of mine, Jimmy Campion. He was one of the thirteen boys who were away from the classroom, helping with the clothing drive. He lived in an apartment on Hamlin, almost across the street from the church, so I went over there with him. After spending some time there, I went home. We lived at Augusta and Hamlin, 3751 Augusta, about half a block away. My mom would leave for work around four o'clock, and she had heard all the sirens. She was worried and getting dressed fast when I came in around 3:45. She was thrilled to see me. My dad wasn't home. He was a truck driver, out on a route. My mom ended up going to work when she saw that I was okay. She had no idea how bad the fire was until later.

I actually went out and delivered my papers that day— the *Chicago American*. They used to drop off the papers in the lower level of the apartment we lived in. I wrapped my forty-five papers and went out and delivered them. When

I came back later, my brother Jack was home. He said he could smell the smoke on me. My dad worked for the truckers union, so we went to the union clinic on Ashland Avenue where a doctor checked me out because I had inhaled so much smoke. It seemed the smoke was radiating out of me. But my checkup turned out okay.

I was one of the lucky ones, that's for sure. There were sixty-three kids in our classroom. Thirteen were out helping Monsignor Cussen with the clothing drive, and two kids were absent. So there were only forty-eight kids in the class at the time of the fire. Twenty-four of them died, and many others were injured quite severely with burns and broken bones.

At home we stayed up really late that night, past midnight, watching television and looking at the list of names of all the kids who died. I remember thinking, "Holy man, these were kids I knew and played with." It was very traumatic, and I had a hard time sleeping after that. So many of my classmates were gone—Larry Grasso, Mary Louise Tamburrino, Millicent Corsiglia, Frances Guzaldo, and Karen Hobik. I was kinda keen on Karen. Some time later, five or six of us survivors visited the father of Frances Guzaldo to offer our sympathy. He was a barber. He wanted us to talk about Frances. He kept her room at their home like a shrine. Frances, Karen, Michele McBride [of Room 209], and myself were members of the student council and helped arrange such events as dances and roller-skating parties.

After the fire I went first for a short time to Our Lady Help of Christians and then to Cameron public school. I attended St. Philip High School at Jackson and Kedzie for a couple of years. My parents, like many others, reluctantly moved out of the neighborhood in December 1959 and settled in St. Ferdinand's Parish around Austin and Belmont. I commuted long distance to St. Philip for a year and a half. My father had died in 1960, and my family talked me into transferring to St. Pat's High School, which was only a couple of blocks away from where we lived.

When I think back on the fire, I admit I never really showed a lot of emotion about it until I read the book *To Sleep with the Angels*. It brought tears to my eyes. It was like I had suppressed memories about what happened. When you're older, you realize how your parents must have felt, how you would have felt if it was one of your kids who died or was injured.

The day after the fire I remember going back to the school to look around. What I saw—all the broken windows, the burned-out section of the north wing, the caved-in roof—made me feel so glad I survived. It is still hard to believe what horrible things happened there.

Sister Mary Donatus
DeCock, B.V.M.

❦

A former teacher at Mundelein College and Loyola University in Chicago, she lives in the Rogers Park neighborhood on the North Side of the city. On the day of the fire she traveled to Our Lady of the Angels convent to lend her assistance to nuns gathered there. "I'm one of the old-timers," she laughs as she mentions she's eighty-five years old. "I've been retired since 1993, though I continued to teach after that." She joined the B.V.M. community in 1944.

I arrived at the scene shortly after the fire had been extinguished. I had been working in the public relations office at Mundelein College; my boss at that time was Dan Cahill. [Mundelein College was then under the administration of the B.V.M. nuns, who also operated twenty-six elementary schools and four high schools in Chicago.] When we got word of the fire, we were asked to go out to Our Lady of the Angels and do anything we could do to help. Firemen were still around when we got there.

I went into the convent, where my job was to keep the press from going in to talk to the Sisters. The entrance to the convent was on Iowa Street, and I became the guardian of the door. Monsignor [William] McManus, superintendent of Catholic schools, did not want the nuns to talk to the media. It was a terrible injustice to the Sisters, because stories came out from different sources, especially from parents, about how angry they were, claiming the Sisters hadn't done anything to save their children. I'm sure they did some dumb things, but they did some good things too. Some of them made mistakes, but what would most of us do in such threatening circumstances? Would we have done things differently?

At the convent the Sisters were all gathered in the community room, working hard to find out which parents had to be notified and trying to figure out what they should do next and how to cope with the tragedy. Stories were floating around that Sister St. Florence, the school principal, was falling apart, which was totally untrue. She wasn't the "falling apart" kind.

It seemed like I stayed at the convent forever. It was very late when we returned to the college. I returned to the convent the next day, and by that time several of the nuns were in the hospital. Sister Helaine, Sister Davidis, and Sister Geraldita had been taken to St. Anne's Hospital. I don't remember where Sister Mary St. Florence was at that point, but the provincial was over there to help her handle it.

At Wright Hall near Mundelein, Sister Carol Frances Jegen was organizing lists to get all the sisters to the wakes and funerals. She said, "We wanted to let all the grieving parents and relatives know how much we cared through our presence and continued prayers." I don't know how she did it, but she managed to have B.V.M. nuns at all the wakes and funerals, getting drivers and listing the different places where the nuns should go. Some of them experienced a sense of discomfort, because nuns were the last people in the world a few of the parents wanted to see at that point. I went to a lot of the wakes myself. It was a very sorrowful experience.

With all the pictures that were in the newspapers or shown on TV, the headdress of the B.V.M. nuns became familiar to many Chicagoans. When we'd travel in pairs on public transportation, you could sense some people would notice our habit and be talking to each other as they looked our way. I have often wished I could have heard what they were saying. It was an odd experience, riding the bus and knowing that people were talking about you.

Our Lady of the Angels fire commanded the nation's attention. Some of the nuns, sadly, got a bad reputation from it because the Fire Department hadn't been called soon enough. Sister Mary St. Florence was never interviewed. She was an excellent principal, but she never had a chance to tell her side of the story. Papers were looking for someone to blame, alleging poor housekeeping, things of that nature. Accusations like that are pretty hard to take when you know how good she was in all aspects and responsibilities of her job. Her statement at the coroner's inquest was very brief. The state's attorney's office did not want to ask her any questions because they thought it would be too hard on her psychologically.

[*On December 11, 1958, at the inquest in the auditorium of the Prudential Building in downtown Chicago, Sister Mary St. Florence was called to the witness stand, but Roy Tuch-*

breiter, foreman of the jury, asked that she be excused after only a few minutes.]

I went to the dedication of the new school in 1960. I really had no desire to go back there. My memories were not very happy ones about what happened there and how it affected our community. I knew Sister Mary St. Florence very well, and also Sister Andrienne, who was a great Irish lady. As time went on, one after another of the Sisters had serious reactions to the school fire. I remember Sister Geraldita Ennis—she was terribly affected by it. You never forget an experience like that. I've never forgotten it, and I did nothing but stand there and talk to people and try to be of help to the other nuns.

That event made me a feminist because of how the Sisters were so mistreated by Monsignor McManus. They never got a chance to tell fully their version of what happened. In newspaper stories, Sister Mary St. Florence came out looking like an incompetent woman. And she was the exact opposite. All of this was because of the restrictions that were placed upon the nuns. Monsignor McManus said quite bluntly that he didn't want to get into any lawsuits. In other words, "those dumb nuns" might say something that would put the archdiocese in a bad legal position. That's the way I interpreted it.

In our B.V.M. community, however, the school fire is a tragedy that will never be forgotten. Some aspects of it weren't handled well by the clergy, but hopefully all of us learned from it.

Bill O'Brien

❧

He lives with his wife Geraldine in Hanover Park, a village some thirty miles west of Chicago. They marked their forty-fifth wedding anniversary in 2008 and have three children and six grandchildren. A repairman of vending machines, he escaped the school fire by jumping to a small roof over a landing below the window of his room facing the courtyard. He then raced to pull the fire alarm box a block away from the school. "I did a lot of running that day," he recalls.

From my perspective, strangely enough, the fire really hasn't affected my life. At the time I was very fortunate that I was the third one out of Room 209 after a couple of the bigger students were able to jump to that small porch overhang below our window. The overhang had some tar paper on it and roofing shingles. The two boys who jumped ahead of me were Ed Maggerise and Jimmy Sturtevant. When I looked back before I jumped, the back door had flames on it already. In those years I was like a little monkey, climbing all over things, and I was able to climb down with no problem. Then I ran through the courtyard and climbed over the metal fence at the front. From there I ran to Chicago

Avenue. There was a fire alarm box on Chicago and Avers, and I remember running over there and pulling the alarm. By then I heard the sirens coming, though.

I then went into Dale's drug store on the corner and yelled that the school was on fire. I recall thinking about my mother being over on Hamlin Avenue, picking up my sister Colleen from kindergarten. So I ran over there, but I didn't see her. I ran back through the alley and back to Avers to the school.

In the next few minutes a few miracles happened. My classmate Jimmy Warzecha was crawling down the street on his hands and knees. He had apparently jumped from some height and injured his legs. He lived on Avers only five or six houses away. So I sort of gave him a piggyback ride to his house and set him down on his stairs. I stayed with him a few minutes, then I went to the corner of Avers and Iowa, where I saw my other sister, Maureen. She was standing there, shivering. She had been in Room 212.

Miracle number one was that a fireman got to that side of the building, put a ladder up to her window first, and pulled her down. She was one of the first ones out of that room. She was fortunate, but she was burned. I didn't re-alize it at the moment, but she was in shock. Smoke was coming out of her nose. So I took her into the convent, right there on Avers and Iowa, got her some water, and sat with her for a minute or so. I told her our mother had to be extremely worried, and that we gotta get home. Our family lived at 657 North Springfield Avenue.

I took her out the back door of the convent, and miracle number two happened. There was a guy in the alley with a station wagon, and he says, "Come on, I'll take you home." Here's a guy looking at all the action going on, and he disregards what's happening to help us. He obviously saw my sister with the smoke and look on her face. I didn't realize it at the time, but her legs were burned from the radiators she was squashed against, by the window of her room. So the man, a perfect stranger, took us home.

We lived on the third floor of our apartment. I got Maureen upstairs and laid her down on the couch, and I said, "I gotta go find our mother." Maureen didn't say anything, but I could see she appeared to be okay to me. So I ran back down the street to look for my mother. I couldn't find her. I went up and down the alley near Hamlin, and around there. I figured, I better get back home, maybe she's there by now. So I ran back to my house and found that my sister was gone. The neighbor lady, Mrs. Wlas, said she saw me helping her upstairs. She came across to our apartment and figured that my sister needed to go to the hospital. Here's miracle number three. She gets an ambulance! With all that commotion going on blocks away, an ambulance came and took my sister to St. Anne's Hospital. Mrs. Wlas lived right across the street from us. She was a Polish lady, a seamstress, a single mother of a friend of mine, Johnny Wlas, who was in seventh grade. She was in a state of commotion too, because her son was in the school.

I finally got together with my mother. She had come home. She was a nervous wreck, of course, but super glad to hear that my sister was alive and in the hospital. Then she got hold of my father and my older sister, Margaret, who was married. My dad was a clerk for a wood service company on the South Side. He didn't get home until about 6 or 6:30 that night. He didn't have a car, so he had to take a couple of buses to get home. He was happy to hear we were okay. Before that, I went across the street to see Mrs. Wlas.

Johnny had come home. We watched the news on TV, and I remember hearing the first reports coming in, that there were seven dead, then nine dead, twenty-one dead. I said, "This is nuts. This is crazy."

The fortunate thing I did not do that day was to go back to the school and see the disaster that was happening on the north end of the building. I didn't see what I heard later, about kids jumping out the windows and being on fire. In Room 209 we were lucky. Only two kids in our room died, Beverly Burda and Valerie Thoma.

I never had a bad dream about the fire. I never needed counseling. I'm sure many, many kids needed some help on that. I don't know why I didn't. I had been an altar boy, and I knew that tragedies happen, but I never needed psychological help. We went back to school the next week and went to Mass on Sunday at the Alamo Theater. Among the kids we hung around with, Michele Altobelli, who was in the other eighth-grade classroom, was the one we lost from our little clique.

After the fire I went to Our Lady Help of Christians and then to John Hay public school. From there I went to Cathedral High School at State and Chicago Avenue. I switched from Cathedral after a year and a half and enrolled at Austin High School. It was such a culture shock coming from a Catholic school that I didn't think I was going to be able to finish high school, so I started working at the Ancona Bakery on Chicago Avenue. I became a baker full time for ten years. I got married in 1963. We were only eighteen when we married, so I didn't get into military service and end up in Vietnam. Because of my allergies, I finally had to get out of the bakery business, and I started driving a truck for Dolly Madison and Holsum Bread. Then a friend of mine who was in the vending business got me another job in the early 1970s. That's what I've been doing ever since.

I've gone to a number of Our Lady of the Angels reunions. Back in 1999 I organized the reunion for the class of '59. We had a great get-together. We had Father Ognibene, and Father McDonnell showed up along with Sister Mary Remi. Father Ognibene, what a guy. He loved children. Eight or nine of my classmates, we met with him right before he passed away. We knew he was dying. He opened up a little bit about the school. He said that things weren't run right. He mentioned the lack of a fire door on the second floor, and he really wished things had been different. He had tears in his eyes talking about all the terrible things that had occurred.

Myself and my classmates who had visited Father Ognibene, we told him we were going to make sure he wasn't forgotten. After he died, the Friends of OLA had a meeting, and I suggested that we build a memorial garden in honor of Father Joe. We didn't know where or how, but the other members approved the suggestion. Later we talked to Father Dan [Fallon], the pastor at Our Lady of the Mother Church, and he agreed it would be a nice idea because Father Joe was once pastor there himself. He said he would okay the spot. I called and interviewed some landscapers and got one to come in with plans, and eventually the garden was built there on Oakview Avenue [now named Father Joe Ognibene Avenue].

When I think back about the fire after all these years, certain memories stay with me. In our room for a short time at the beginning of the fire there was a real strange silence—and then the girls were screaming and crying. Everybody seemed to be like zombies, walking around, bumping into each other, and looking at the ceiling. Sister Davidis said we should say the rosary. That's when I decided this is not going to work, and I propelled myself over to the back window. When I watched those two guys jump, I thought, if they can do it, I can do it too. There were still some sixty kids behind me. I was a little guy, and I still don't know what kind of miracle it took to get me into a spot where I could get out without injury.

My sister Maureen and I, we didn't talk about our experiences in the fire for many, many years. She was about twenty-six or so, I was about thirty. We started talking then, asking each other, do you remember this, do you remember that? She remembers watching her best friend, Antoinette Secco, die. She saw her collapse. After we were able to talk about it, we realized that life goes on. We felt a little closer. I was not her hero at that moment, but she was my heroine. I could still envision her, standing on that corner with no coat on, shaking from the cold, and with the smoke all around her nose and mouth. It's one of those things that stay with you. I don't know how I would have reacted if she had been hurt worse, like Gerry Andreoli and Michele McBride who were in my room.

At one of the anniversary Masses we met with Cardinal George and discussed with him briefly the possibility of erecting a memorial to the nuns and students who died in the fire. He agreed to it. There was a meeting downtown with Bishop Edwin Conway, whose parents were once parishioners at Our Lady of the Angels. It was decided at that meeting to have the memorial and use the statue of Our Lady that was in the garden of the old rectory. We had a stand built for it with all the names engraved in gold. We dedicated it in 2000. That day, December 1, they were delivering the finished memorial, so I drove over there in my work van. I pulled up in front of the new school on Iowa Street. They were lifting the memorial off the back of a truck. So I parked my van in front of their truck and held the door of the school open for the guys to carry the memorial into the vestibule where they set it on the floor. They put the statue on top of the base, and we were standing there admiring it. A little later I walked outside with Father [Nicholas] Desmond, and guess what? My van was gone! It was stolen! I had taken my keys with me. They jumped the ignition. They evidently had seen the vending logo on the side of the van and must've thought there were a lot of products or money inside.

It was just another sign of how much the neighborhood had changed from the days when we used to play on the streets there as kids, and adults didn't have to worry about crime being so mean and prevalent, and there weren't any police security cameras on light posts.

John Lubke

*He and his younger brother were both injured in escaping
fire-ravaged rooms at Our Lady of the Angels. A graduate
of the University of Notre Dame, he operates his own CPA
firm and resides with his wife, Daina, in Glenview, Illinois,
in a house which he says, with a sense of humor, is a big
upgrade from the apartment where he lived as the son of
working parents in his growing-up days.*

What happened to me that day made me appreciate being alive, made me realize we should enjoy life, not take
it for granted, and that you'd better enjoy every damn day
because it's not guaranteed. It gave me the drive to "go for
it" all the time. It woke me up at an early age. I was thirteen
then.

I don't reflect too much on the school fire today, unless
the subject comes up when I meet with someone from the
old neighborhood. I did have nightmares about it the first
year or so, but nothing since then. In my era you didn't
have all the counseling they have today.

I had two paper routes at the time. I delivered the *Chicago American*. I was out of action for about a month, so

the kid who had my southern route told everyone I'd died. In those days you collected the money from the customers on your route. So the first week I got back, I went to this little old lady's house and knocked on her door to collect my money. When she opens the door, she screams, "A ghost!" And she hits the deck. I shout, "Lady, it's really me!" I was flabbergasted. I didn't know why she thought I was gone.

My folks lived then at 926 North Harding. There were three kids in the family, two boys and a girl. My brother Fred was in fourth grade, on the alley side of the school. He was the last kid to get out of his room before the roof collapsed. He had just got on a ladder when the roof came down behind him. The flames gushed out and burned his hands and ears. He was only ten years old. He was taken to Franklin Boulevard Hospital and was there for about three weeks.

My room [211] was on the other side of the north wing, facing the courtyard. When the smoke came into the room, everybody panicked. The nun [Sister Helaine] sort of fell apart. We weren't told to drop and crawl. In hindsight, we could've crawled to the staircase that was only about ten feet from our front door and gone down to the Avers Street exit. If we'd covered our faces and done that immediately, even if we staggered, we all would've gotten out alive. But the nun said, "Say the Act of Contrition." And, the bad guys in the class said, "F this, get us out of here." The smoke just scared you, and you looked to the nun for leadership, but it wasn't there. In retrospect it was stupidity up and down the line.

So then we rushed to the windows. I remember I was lying on the window ledge, trying to breathe because the smoke was terrible and everybody was piled on top of me.

I'll go to my grave remembering this: a kid crawled out onto the ledge and just stepped into space like he was walking down the sidewalk. I turned my head. I didn't want to see him when he hit the cement in the courtyard.

Then I felt my ass getting hot from the flames, and I thought, "Oh oh, it's time to get out, one way or the other. If I kill myself falling, I kill myself falling." So I wiggled like a snake to get out from under the mass of kids on top of me. When I got free, I somersaulted into the air and hit the ground. I went right out. I remember I bounced three times. I was semi-conscious after I landed on the cement. I'd pass out and wake up, and pass out again. A priest who was there kept giving me last rites. I had hurt my elbow and my back. It seems like the real nice kids in our classroom died and the wild ones got out. John Trotta, who died, would've grown up to be a scientist or a doctor.

At Franklin Boulevard Hospital my arm was in a sling. When it came time for x-rays, a big nurse just straightened my elbow, and boy did I yell. On the anniversary of the fire they sometimes show a tape on television of injured kids at a hospital. In one scene there's a kid being brought in on a stretcher, and I'm 99 percent sure that's me.

Today I still feel the aftereffects of my fall in the court-yard. I've got a bum back. I still can't come anywhere close to touching my toes.

Looking back, I think the inquest into the fire was a sham. The jury didn't determine its cause or origin. They wanted to cover it up. They didn't want the church black-ened. Even the nuns wouldn't let us talk about it when we went back to school. It's just the opposite nowadays. In those days you didn't sue the church, you didn't fight it. My dad was a mean old German, and he wanted to sue, but my mother said, "Oh, no, no, you don't sue the church." They were factory workers. My dad worked at Schwinn Bicycle, my mother worked at Motorola. They were blue-collar. As a kid I didn't know what that meant.

Here's what the school fire taught me: I tell young guys all the time, "Go for it. Ask the prettiest girl to dance. Drink the last drink. You might be dead before you know it. What are you worried about?" I wound up successful in life, became a CPA, have two wonderful daughters, and went to Notre Dame, which was beyond my wildest dreams when I was growing up. Both my daughters, Angie and Natalie, also went to Notre Dame, were on the dean's list, and graduated from there. As the son of two hourly wage earners, I take pride in that. And in view of what happened to me so many years ago, I have to say I'm most thankful to be alive.

Bob Wiedrich

A well-known Chicago Tribune *reporter and columnist for more than forty years, he drove through stoplights in his rush to get to the site of the school fire. He was thirty-one at the time. Today he and his wife, Margery, live on the North Side of the city. In his retirement he says with a laugh, "I don't play golf. I don't chase fire engines. If I don't have something to do, I just go stir crazy."*

Each city room in the Chicago daily newspapers had instruments identical to the ones that rang alarms in all the Fire Department houses. We had a card file, listing box numbers for schools and other types of important locations. The minute the school alarm rang in the office, the day city editor, Harold Murray, told me to get out there. We had looked up the nearby box, found the address of the school and the name of it. I just jumped in my car and drove like a crazy man to Our Lady of the Angels. I went straight west on Chicago Avenue. I broke every traffic rule under the sun, ran all the traffic lights. I got there when kids were still jumping out the windows. I saw two of them go out. The scene I was confronted with was terrible.

After the worst part was over, Walter McCarron, the Cook County coroner, appeared at the school, followed a little later by Mayor Richard J. Daley. I grabbed McCarron by the arm and said, "You're going to take me in there." I wanted to look inside the rooms. He said, "I ain't goin' in there." And I said, "Yes, you are, and you're taking me with you." I knew the police and fire guys wouldn't let me in the building by myself.

So I went in with McCarron, and while it gave me a helluva story, I was never so sorry I made that decision. It was just an absolutely horrible disaster in there. On the second floor was a room where some kids who died were still at their desks. The nun who had been seated at the front of the room was lying flat over her own desk, as if she had been knocked down by the flames. She was horribly burned, and it appeared to me she was sprawled over her desk as if she was trying to reach out and protect some of the kids. The dead kids, the smell, the water dripping . . . it was a sight I'll never forget.

It was the first and only time I ever saw Mayor Daley cry. I stood beside him in front of the school after I came out with McCarron, and the two of us were blubbering like a couple of kids. It was just a gut-wrenching heartbreaker. As bad as it was in that school, the late George Bliss [another *Tribune* reporter] had the worst assignment of the day. He had to go to the County Morgue and wait there with the parents to identify their children. I don't think George ever recovered from that.

On the west side of Avers Avenue there were houses occupied by parents who had children in the school. Despite all the horror, I went across the street and with other reporters asked these people if we could use their phones.

And they let us. I called the office, and they told me to come in and write the story. Fred Farrar, who was a young *Tribune* reporter, had been sent out maybe an hour after the fire started. He did whatever the hell he had to do. Then I met up with him and said, "Come on, I've gotta have a drink." I had parked on Chicago Avenue, a block south of the school, and had run like crazy the rest of the way because I couldn't get my car any closer. We went back and found my car. There was a saloon on the corner. I went in there and drank four or five straight shots of scotch and didn't feel a goddam thing. It was weird. I should've been bombed and I wasn't.

I left Fred there to do the cleanup stuff, and I drove back to the paper. Right in the middle of writing the story, I broke down. But I got it done, and it ran on page one of the replate edition around six or seven o'clock. In later editions they were able to publish pictures on the front page of the children who had died, and my story was moved to page three. I'm eighty-one now. I've seen war, I've seen executions, I've seen every miserable happening in life, but the school fire was the worst I ever saw. These innocent little kids, all burned, scrunched over their desks . . . it was horrible.

In 1962 I covered the Juvenile Court hearing for the boy who set the fire. They closed the hearing to most everybody but reporters, and we had to swear that we'd never reveal the boy's name. He was the result of an incestuous relationship between his mother and her father, so that his grandfather was his real father. His mother had married a tradesman of some sort. I don't remember what. And the guy was a helluva man. He thought the kid was the result of an earlier marriage. Then while he's sitting there during testimony in the court hearing he finds out about this incestuous relationship. But he stuck by that kid. He didn't walk out on him. Eventually they decided to send the boy to an out-of-state juvenile center.

When I think about the school fire, too often it's like it happened yesterday. I still get emotional about it. I hope I never see anything like that again. During the war I was in combat and I saw deaths, but not in multiples like at the school. Memories of those dead kids never leave me.

The following article, bearing Robert Wiedrich's byline, appeared in the Chicago Tribune *on Tuesday, December 2, 1958:*

Six small forms, the bodies of fourth or fifth graders, lay crumpled against the wall.

In the corner, the charred body of a nun lay buried in debris of the roof which had fallen into the room.

A fireman hacked at the wreckage of a second-floor classroom in the Our Lady of the Angels elementary school. Tears streaked his smoke-smeared face. "Oh, God, I've got two of my own in school," he said. "What if these were mine?"

In another room, the desks stood row on row. Each bore a waterlogged geography book. It was called *Our American Neighbors*. Each was open to the chapter on lumbering.

This was the aftermath of a fire so hot and so swift that several score young lives were taken in a matter of minutes as rescuers worked as fast as they could, but found that it was not fast enough.

The porcelain figure of the Virgin Mary stood on a bookcase. It had been a planter. The leaves of the plant were mere ashes. And the statue looked out over a room of death. The water-soaked papers of a child working on an arithmetic problem lay on a desk. The ink had run and the figures were blurred. The paper would never be graded. The teacher was dead. So was the pupil. You could see where both had sought to flee the searing heat of the fire.

The nun's desk had been hurled forward as she struggled to reach her charges in the final agony of flame. And the pupil's small body was by the desk, his features contorted.

A battalion chief sloshed through the water that flowed on the concrete floor. He said he had been one of the first at the scene. He wept as he told how firemen had tried to raise ladders to screaming children as they clung to second-floor windows, pleading for the help which, for many, never came. "We tried," he said. "God, how we tried. But, we couldn't move fast enough. No one could live in that fire.

"I saw four of them leaning over a windowsill, crying. We tried to reach them. Then, suddenly they slumped, doubled over the sill. They were dead when we got to them."

The school's second floor was burned out, wall to wall. Sections of the roof collapsed. A wool mitten, decorated with sequins, lay in the rubble.

Twenty more minutes and the children would have been out of school; 1,200 seconds and death would have been cheated. The blaze struck at 2:40 p.m. Classes ended at 3 p.m.

Firemen stumbled over the wooden desks that stood in a double line in the second-floor corridor. "The ones who jumped were lucky," said a division marshal. "They just broke arms and legs. I hope I never see something like this again."

Outside the school, parents stood. Priests knelt to give the last rites to canvas-covered forms that once had been children. Mothers wept and fathers tried to comfort, but cried, too.

On Chicago Avenue, a block to the south, a loudspeaker blared Christmas carols from the door of a record shop. But Christmas in this neighborhood would be grim.

In Our Lady of the Angels Church, just east of the school, the lights were out. Fire had burned the power lines. But in the pitch-black church, people knelt and prayed, the bitter smell of smoke in their nostrils. And on the steps, a woman cried. A cold wind swirled the smoke from the still smoldering school about her.

Dan Lupo

For years he has considered his Aunt Joan his guardian angel. He was born December 1, 1958, within hours of her death at age ten in Room 210 of Our Lady of the Angels School. He now lives in Austin, Texas, with his wife and daughter, serves as a hospice chaplain, and is a deacon candidate in the Austin diocese.

My mother Margaret was in St. Elizabeth Hospital giving birth to me when my dad heard news of the school fire on a radio in the waiting room. My mother was the big sister of Joan Chiappetta. There were quite a few years between them. My dad asked the doctor if he thought it would be okay to tell my mom of the tragic news. He knew that her younger sister was in the school but didn't know if she had survived. The doctor told him not to tell my mom because she was weak and had lost a lot of blood delivering me. So my dad asked my mother's hospital roommate, who had just received a new radio, not to play it for a while.

Then my dad and my uncle, Ernie Chiappetta, who was my mother's brother, went to the school to look for the kids, my aunt and two uncles, Bob and Arthur, who were also students. They couldn't even get close to the scene and were told to go to the Cook County Morgue. They went, but they couldn't make any identifications. They went to St. Anne's Hospital with the same outcome. They headed back home and decided to try again later. This time my aunt, Rosemary Chiappetta, went with them to the morgue and was able to identify Joanie by a locket she was wearing that had been given to her by my mom and dad.

Growing up, I was never aware of the bittersweet nature of my birthday. As far as I knew, my birthday was my birthday and that was that. All the grief of that day never clouded my birthday celebrations. I was just a kid. I was oblivious of what had happened and the impact it had on so many families. It was only when I was older that I learned about December 1 being not only my birthday but also the day my aunt had perished. I am amazed and grateful that my mom and dad and extended family could hide so well their pain and sadness from me all those years.

In our house, as I grew up, there was a picture of Aunt Joanie and her siblings. It was an oil painting. In that picture, Joanie had brown hair and big, brown, almost sad, eyes. Her smile was weak, forced, almost as if she were unaccustomed to smiling.

In late fall of 2001 I had a reached a low point in my life. I hit a midlife crisis. Things were not going well, and most of the mess was of my making. I was feeling empty and wondering, "Well, here I am, I'm married, I got a kid, I've got this high-tech job. What else is there to life? What is this thing called life all about? Why am I here?" I was asking myself these basic questions that we don't spend much time thinking about except in the few quiet moments we allow ourselves. The bombing of the Twin Towers in New

York had just happened. I started questioning a lot of stuff. I felt powerless. I could have easily buried myself in work or turned to alcohol or just blown everything off, but for whatever reason I turned to prayer. In my prayers I asked God for help.

My wife, Joanne, suggested we attend a reconciliation service at St. Thomas More Church in Austin, Texas. When the priest asked us to kneel to review our consciences, I looked inside myself and saw nothing . . . only blackness, utter emptiness. I felt alone, afraid, helpless. I did the only thing I could do. I prayed. I asked God's help in turning my life around.

When I opened my eyes and stood up, I saw something out of the corner of my eye. I looked and a little girl who sat sideways was looking directly at me. The girl looked exactly like my Aunt Joanie from the portrait I remembered hanging in our house when I was growing up in the Portage Park area of Chicago. Her likeness was so amazingly similar to my aunt's that I was moved to tell my wife. I whispered, "Look at that little girl. She looks exactly like my aunt who died the day I was born."

As I said these words, a thought came to me: "Maybe this *is* my aunt. Maybe she is my guardian angel. Maybe God is responding to my prayers, revealing his presence in my life through my guardian angel and telling me he has been helping me all along via my guardian angel, my Aunt Joanie." My reaction was visceral. I knew it as soon as I said to myself, "This must be my guardian angel." Although it amazed me, this revelation felt real and true to me. It was a powerful experience. On the drive home I struggled to articulate to my wife what I was feeling. The next day I shared my experience with my parents on the phone. They both assured me. They said, "We always thought that Joanie was your guardian angel."

Since that time my life has turned completely around. I have been led on a journey of discovering the truth of God's mercy and love. My heart has been opened to allow me to see that love courses through our lives and is as easily accessible as a kind word or gesture to another human being. Pray, love, serve. That's the motto by which I live my life now. Through the deacon formation program I'm now engaged in, I will continue to touch many lives, and my Aunt Joanie will continue to guide me.

Although she may have died in the Our Lady of the Angels fire, Joanie was transformed and became my guardian angel. I believe this firmly. Her blessed innocence lives on in my life and in turn touches all the people I encounter.

Raymond Orozco, Jr.

🥀

*The son of former Chicago Fire Commissioner Raymond
Orozco, Sr., he rose through the ranks after beginning
his career as a firefighter in 1980. He advanced to fire
engineer in 1987, to lieutenant assigned to various
Chicago neighborhoods in 1988, to captain in 1993, and
to battalion chief in 1996. He was appointed the city's Fire
Commissioner by Mayor Richard M. Daley in 2006.*

It's a shame it took an event like Our Lady of the Angels
School fire to bring about the changes that have helped us
ensure fire safety in our public and private schools. From
a fire-protection standpoint, what I've seen during my time
on the street as a fireman, as a company officer, as a battalion chief, the schools in the city today are very well run.

There have been so many changes made over the last
fifty years, I really don't see a glaring issue regarding fire
safety in our schools. I can think of only a handful of times
in the almost thirty years that I went out and did fire drills
and actually saw something that could be construed as a
violation in a school.

They're cooking in schools today, they're feeding the kids, something they didn't do years ago. Obviously that's a concern to the department. But such operations are very well maintained by the public schools and some of the private schools that do the cooking.

There's no one special concern regarding fire safety in the schools that jumps off the table at me, and that's because of the changes made since the Our Lady of the Angels tragedy. Members of the department are in the schools a lot, checking things out. What we do, too, is utilize technology.

Any time we answer a call to a school, we get a printout of information about the school. We know how many children are there and the hours of operation, because so many schools have extended activities today. They aren't just functioning from 8 or 9 a.m. to 3 in the afternoon any more. We know when we're going there, even at eight o'clock at night, that we could have anywhere from fifty to a hundred or even more students still in the school. So what we've done, under the mayor's direction, is to gather all this information about the schools and, using technology, push it out to the first responders even before they leave their fire stations.

The school principals are very good about fire drills. The company officer will go in and tell the principal, "We'd like to do a fire drill." If we get the okay from the principal, we time the drill, give the principal some feedback, and then do a blocked-exit drill. We have one of the firefighters stand at a doorway and say, "Okay, this exit is blocked. What's your alternative exit so you can get out?" We do that to see how well prepared the teachers and students are.

Today, if anyone in a school pulls a fire alarm or calls 911, the response will bring four engines, two truck companies, and a battalion chief. The response has changed significantly over the years. On occasion a 911 call will result in a false alarm because so many kids have cell phones. Now the alarm system is directly tied in with the dispatch center on Madison Street. New technology includes cameras deployed throughout the city. The Board of Education has cameras too, so if a fire- or police-related event occurs in a school, we're able to view those cameras and get a look at the scene well before any fire engines get there.

There's no delay today in our response to a school alarm like there was at Our Lady of the Angels. Everything is a hard-wired system. The Chicago Fire Department probably has the best response time of any large department in the United States.

All these technical improvements have provided greater fire safety in our schools. To my knowledge, I don't think there's been a fatality because of fire in a Chicago school since Our Lady of the Angels.

What we have now that we didn't have in 1958 are the added colleges and universities with their dormitories. We can't overlook that group. We go into the dormitories and do drills right there. We go in at ten o'clock at night, four o'clock in the morning—because during the day the students are all in classes. We've also produced a Digital Video Disc on fire safety because all the kids look at DVDs about dorm safety. And we've done that with all the universities and colleges that have campus housing in the city of Chicago.

So we not only take care of the preschools, the grammar schools, and the high schools, but also the colleges.

We went after the college dormitories because nationwide that's where most of the increase in fires and fire deaths have occurred. Instead of waiting for something to happen here in Chicago, we've taken a very preemptive approach in educating that group of people about the dangers of fire.

As commissioner I spent a portion of my time going out to various schools and talking to the students about fire safety. We have a public education unit now, so we're in the schools a lot.

There's no question that what happened at Our Lady of the Angels half a century ago set the wheels in motion for improved fire safety in our schools.

Epilogue

D espite the passing of so many years, most all of those who had connections to the tragedy cling tenaciously to their memories of the Our Lady of the Angels School fire. This became obvious to me through the words of those I talked with, some of whom for the first time spoke publicly about their personal experiences, feelings, and reflections about the fire.

What stood out in conversations with former students was the close bond many have retained with their grammar-school friends, primarily because they were all part of a traumatic event that marked their young lives. Excluding the ravenous cruelty of the fire, however, the majority of them still look back with fondness on more carefree days they spent in the old working-class neighborhood surrounding their school and church. Some admitted that talking about that dreadful December afternoon in 1958 had a therapeutic effect on them. Nonetheless some people were reluctant to revive memories of their actions that day.

Dan Bodnar was a young member of Truck 26, one of the first Fire Department units to arrive amid the chaos taking place. "It's something I can't handle," he said when asked for his recollections.

Pearl Tristano was a twenty-four-year-old lay teacher who led her pupils in Room 206 to safety. She also demurred. "Most of the book," she said, "should be about the former students and how they have moved on with their lives as best they could."

In the years since the catastrophe, many eyewitnesses, including teachers, firefighters, policemen, parish clergy, local residents, and passersby who rushed to the scene, have died, reducing the numbers of people who might provide additional firsthand accounts of what transpired from the time the fire was first detected until it was extinguished.

Four B.V.M. nuns who were teaching in second-floor rooms assaulted by flames and smoke that day are no longer with us, including Sister Helaine O'Neill, who died at seventy-three in 1975; Sister Geraldita Ennis, seventy-five, in 1997; Sister Andrienne Carolan, eighty-one, in 1999; and Sister Davidis Devine, one hundred, in 2006. Sister Helaine succumbed at St. Anne's Hospital, where years before she had been treated for burns; the other nuns passed away at the B.V.M. motherhouse in Dubuque, Iowa.

While gun violence on school premises in recent years has captured the public's attention, statistics on fires in the nation's educational facilities warn that vigilance will always be needed to prevent what may now be regarded as a lesser peril to students.

According to a recent survey by the National Fire Protection Association, between 2002 and 2005 there was an annual average of 6,500 "structure fires" in educational properties, excluding dormitories and fraternity or sorority houses, in the United States. One of five of these fires was intentionally set. Forty-three percent occurred in middle or high schools; 21 percent occurred in elementary schools, including kindergartens. An annual average of 95 civilian injuries and $99 million in property damage resulted from these fires.

Leading causes of the blazes involved cooking, heating, or lighting equipment, as well as accumulated trash or rubbish. Most civilian injuries and property damage, however, were the result of intentionally set fires.

"In Chicago," says Deputy Commissioner of Fire Prevention Larry Muse, "we look after 1,046 schools, some 700 of them in the public school system.

"We regulate day-care centers that house preschool kids a little more strictly than we do the public schools. They have to have their own alarm system. We do fire drills in the day-cares just like we do in the public schools. We're out there every day going to day-cares, elementary schools, whatever, to make sure they're safe.

"In our in-service program, the companies go out and do the fire drills. If for some reason they can't do the drills after two visits, they refer the difficulty back to the Fire Prevention school section, and we send an inspector out to do the drill.

"We do the drills once a month at the schools, depending, of course, on the weather. If it's below twenty degrees, we don't do it unless we're aware of a problem in the school. We don't want the children getting sick. We can't do it if the kids are at lunch or are taking tests, but we like to stick with the once-a-month pattern.

"A big issue, with the shootings that have occurred recently, is to get the principals and teachers to understand that you can't just lock the doors. You must have access to all the doors.

"After the Our Lady of Angels fire, the city enacted an ordinance to sprinkle the older school buildings, so today, any school building that is two stories of ordinary construction or higher has a sprinkler system."

A NOTE ON THE AUTHOR

John Kuenster, a former staff writer and columnist for the *Chicago Daily News*, has also been sports editor of the *New World* and editor of *The Columbian*. He is now executive editor of Lakeside Publishing Company in Evanston, Illinois. He has written extensively for newspapers and magazines. His books include *At Home and Away*, *Heartbreakers*, *The Best of Baseball Digest*, and, with David Cowan, *To Sleep with the Angels*, the story of the Our Lady of the Angels School fire, which has received wide acclaim. He lives with his wife in Evergreen Park, Illinois.